"Roxanne Parks is one of the most ex
humans I know! Now in her new bo
ING DEVOTIONALS, she yet again ... . er-
fervesce some of that exuberant, joyful life-breath into others! We all
need oxygen to live, but if we want to live a life of *joyful impact,* we
need to learn how to become generators of hope and this is what Roxanne dishes out in spades in her devotionals - a veritable "how to"
manual on how to become that person whose very existence breathes
life into the surrounding atmosphere for others. Thank you, Roxanne!
You've done it again!"

-Wes Lane

Founder & Chief Visionary Officer, SALLT
(Salt and Light Leadership Training)
Former Oklahoma District Attorney

"Does the pace you're keeping feel overwhelming? Do you wonder if
there's a better way? If you long for some space to breathe in the grace
of God and drink deeply of the freedom Christ died to give you, this
book is for you. Roxanne Parks has a true gift for encouraging women
through words, and in *BREATHE: 101 LIFE-GIVING DEVOTION-
ALS,* that's exactly what she does. No matter what you're facing right
now, Roxanne's words will breathe new life and hope into your daily
routine and remind you God is interested in meeting you right where
you're at."

-Heidi St. John

Author, Speaker, Podcaster and
Founder of MomStrong International

"Roxanne Parks knows how to slow dance with God! In order to hear the gentle whispers of our Father, you must get close enough and listen. Roxanne knows the heartbeat of God and communicates His truth and grace to thousands of women in America. This writing is a precious sampling of a lifetime of slow dancing with God! Everyone should read and enjoy the compilation of a life well lived for our Savior. I offer my highest possible recommendation to *BREATHE: 101 LIFE-GIVING DEVOTIONALS!*"

-Boe Parrish

Chairman and President, Corporate Care, Inc.

"In *BREATHE: 101 LIFE-GIVING DEVOTIONALS* Roxanne has captured the daily struggles standing in the way of a closer relationship with God for many women. The book provides real, tangible, and meaningful validation of the limits we place on ourselves through comparison and self-doubt and how God provides the tools to move past the pain and draw closer to Him. If you are seeking better relationships with God and those you love, including yourself, this book is for you."

-AJ Griffin

Director of Government and Community Affairs, Paycom
Former Oklahoma State Senator

ROXANNE PARKS

Breathe

ROXANNE PARKS

Breathe

101 Life Giving Devotionals

DEDICATION

*T*his book is dedicated, once again, to my husband, best friend and life-long lover, Bryan Parks. I can't imagine life without you. I treasure that we, as teammates, have WORKED at our marriage and our love for thirty-five years now. I am so grateful for your humility and dedication to this greater work. Your opposite giftings truly have blessed our marriage in places where I am inadequate. You are the most stable, humble and supportive man I know. I love you dearly.

And to my greatest teachers, our children: Matthew, Lauren, David (with Hannah and Dawson) and Jonathan. Each one of you continue to inspire me to be better and understand this next generation. I am inspired by the way you live, full of faith, full of life, full of adventure! I love watching you all make the world a better place. Shine on!

ACKNOWLEDGEMENTS

*P*enny Shaida, my main YouVersion Bible plan editor. Thank you for serving in your "gifting" to bless me and the body of Christ. You work with a servant's heart. I admire you and your grammar skills.

To my other Bible plan editors: **Paula Greenlaw, Ingrid Lewis** and **Andrea Pflughoft.** I am so glad that your skills are not my skills. I needed each correction. I needed you then and, as close friends, I still need you now.

Bekah Goodwin Nichols, who offered to update my brand and marketing strategy when I didn't even have one; that was humbling and laughable. I love that you love making me shine for His greater glory. You are the "icing on my cake."

DeeAnn Higgins, my recent "ministry partner" and always an iron for sharpening. You consistently say just the right things to me at the right time…to build, encourage and edify my heart. You've added so much value to our DEEPER INTENSIVE getaways. I am excited to start our RISE UP: YOUR TIME IS NOW coaching events together.

The girls in my team, tribe and life-group, (you know who you are) who have navigated years of life with me. We have learned so much by living, growing and serving beside each other. Life is always better with you ladies by my side. Each of you inspire me in different ways as only the body of Christ can.

A special acknowledgement to **Suzanne Baxter** as one of my life "besties." Your willingness to listen to me verbally process things so that I could solve my own problems was incomparable. Your steadfast faithfulness to prayer and serving others was the groundwork of your character. I have always been inspired by the sweet way that you loved me unconditionally. It was hard to let you go after our twenty-year friendship. Heaven got you sooner than I wanted, but I look forward to spending eternity with you.

And, finally, to the **Cedar Gate Publishing team**, especially Randy Allsbury, Holden Hill, and Jessica Dodson Stubbs. Your uncanny ability to pull great stories out of others, for greater kingdom glory, is inspiring. I loved working with your creative minds and laughing while we did so.

It is truly an honor to ever be the "hands and feet" of Christ in the lives of another person. My passion is to speak life-giving truths into the hearts of others, and I consider it a humble privilege to do so. Thank you, Lord!

TABLE OF CONTENTS

FOREWORD

*D*ear reader, I am so happy for you. Right now, you have made a life-giving choice. You are holding a cheerleader, a Barnabas (an encourager), in your hands. Our sister, Roxanne, has done the long and good work of growing and maturing in her faith and has given us this book with the goal of powerful, Biblical Truth to help us learn how to breathe deeply, freely, and full of joy.

Does this sound like a trite promise that's too good to be true? Maybe. Maybe not. To me, it's all about if we will choose to put the Truth into practice.

I recently watched the labor and birth of our grandson, Jace, by our second daughter, Mandy. Oh, and she had him naturally at home with a midwife. It was absolutely beautiful and miraculous! Proper breathing was a critical part of the process. Apparently, not all breathing is the same or gives the same results. Mandy's breath needed to be deep (not shallow) and through the nose. Mouth-breathing or yelling through a contraction was not going to benefit her or the baby.

I was so proud of her. Giving birth to an eight-pound baby certainly wasn't easy, but Mandy had a greater purpose than her current pain. Whenever she began to holler or her breathing got out of control, she listened intently to her coach, the expert midwife, and would immediately change her behavior. I'm pretty sure her husband, James, and I were simultaneously adjusting our breathing as well. If this is making you feel a little tense right now, just stop for a moment with me and take a deep breath… All better? Whew!

Maybe there's something for us to learn from this example? Maybe there's a better way for us to breathe?

What I appreciate about Roxanne is that she doesn't sugarcoat the harsh realities of life. Quite the opposite, she hits our everyday battles head-on and shows us how to lean fully on God and His empowering Breath instead of our own.

I believe you'll see yourself in these pages.

Roxanne's encouraging spirit is contagious. Her relatable experiences will make you laugh, sigh, and maybe even cry. Personally, I've watched in amazement as Roxanne has weathered storms with unshakeable confidence and unworldly peace. But she will be the first to stand up and enthusiastically declare that its because of the life of the Holy Spirit living inside her that made all the difference and helped her breathe with abundant life.

I pray this book will help you do the same.

—Amy Groeschel

INTRODUCTION

*H*ave you ever had days where you feel like you are about to suffocate under the stress and burdens of a full life? Do you ever feel like no matter how much you love God and others, you still struggle with feeling like a failure as a mom, wife, and friend at times? Do you ever feel as though the life you're living is not how life was supposed to be? Do you need some extra oxygen for your soul?

I once knew a woman who came home every night and saw dishes piled up, kids who were illusive and distant, and a spouse with whom she couldn't connect. She was overwhelmed by the very life that she had dreamed about. She carried a lingering feeling that she didn't have what it took to balance all that was on her plate. Surely she wasn't enough. She felt like a failure as a mom, a wife, and a manager of her home. How could this be?

I also knew a woman who had such a heart for the Lord and His work but seemed to always find herself so distracted from what mattered most as she was drowning in the immediate and the urgent. She valued quality time with her family, her personal fitness, and time to meditate on scripture but found herself buried in mundane things like laundry and dishes. Her heart was purely set on her priorities, but her days were filled with taunting distractions.

A few years earlier, I knew a sensitive woman who seemed to live offended by the poor behaviors of "those" people in her life. Once she heard her friend speak critically behind her back and she could never shake the offense. The offense penetrated her soul, but she yearned to not live offended and separated from her friend or her people. Was she strong enough to navigate harshness in others? She needed tougher skin.

Or the woman who spent too many days racing on the performance treadmill in an exhausting race with herself and those she compared herself with. She had a resume full of empty titles that proved her ability, but her plates were always spinning and often falling to the ground. She wondered if all this was just an effort in futility. Was it all a "vanity of vanity" as is written in Ecclesiastes? Or a "chasing after the wind"? She was desperately seeking a true and intimate rest for her soul, not just a rest from her activities.

And lastly, I knew a woman who was overwhelmed by all the voices going through her head leading to all the choices that she needed to make. Should she do it this way or that way? Yes or no? Now or later? With them or others? Scold them or not? So many choices! So many voices. Which decision was the right decision to make? Anxiety became her norm. She was sinking into a depression from the overwhelm of the noise.

Actually, guess what? All those women mentioned above are me!

Do you find yourself struggling in any of these same ways? Do you have any friends like this? A life full of blessings and a life full of confusion?

Here are other questions that have been on my mind that might be on your mind as well:

- I know that marriage matters, but how can I make it to "death do you part" with my perfectly imperfect spouse?

- How can I reconcile the power of life-giving words when sometimes my own mouth betrays me as I speak out of anger, pain, or discouragement?

- How can the thoughts that I think lead me to a life of gratitude and power?

- Is there a way for my control freak to die in the moment so that I can live for the greater purpose? Where do I get this strength?

- Is there anything in me worthy of blessing this world and leaving a legacy that matters? Is my life significant and does my life truly count?

- I am so confused and unsure! If there is a true wisdom to be had, where can I find it?

- How should I pray to a God that I can often feel distant from?

- Can I make it through raising children when my enemy wants to steal, kill, and destroy their purposes through teenage confusion?

If you have struggled with these or similar questions, then these devotionals are just for you. It is straight from the heart of God to my heart, and straight from my heart to your heart. Share it with others as your heart wants to encourage them as well. These devotional thoughts are a result of decades of lifelong learning which turned into workshops and retreat topics. Then, more recently, this information turned into YouVersion Bible plans. Now we have compiled it together in one book to build and speak life-giving truths into your weary and beautiful heart.

Join me in learning to breathe from the very breath of God. Zechariah 4:6 states, "Not by my power, nor by my might BUT by the **Spirit** of the Lord." The indwelling Spirit gives us the power to live FROM His wisdom and strength versus the daily exhaustion of living FOR Him. It is 100 percent up to God to empower us to live in His will, in His way … BUT it is 100 percent up to us to yield and invite Him to do so.

I invite you to breathe in the Holy Spirit power that has been given to you in order to live from the place of freedom and rest that is your Christian privilege … Christ in you, the hope of glory! Tether your heart and your peace of mind to the character of God and not to this world, the news, other people, or circumstances.

Do you want to breathe deeply, peacefully, joyfully, and fully alive?

Come, and let's receive the Lord's breath together!

CHAPTER 1

An Unoffendable Heart

Have you ever felt offended? Was that just today or yesterday? Years ago, I asked the Lord to show me all the places that I had an "offendable heart." I thought this would be an exercise in Christian maturity. Little did I know. Never could I have realized the extent to which there are opportunities to take offense until I opened my eyes to see. Today, I can recognize an "offendable heart" so quickly. In myself. In others. Taking offense is rampant on the news, on social media, and in our homes. An easily offendable heart destroys relationships. Let's not go there!

Day 1

Taking Offense

*O*ffense can be defined as something that outrages the moral or physical senses, the act of displeasing or affronting. Everyone is certain to feel offended at one point or another. The problem with living offended is that it doesn't hurt someone else … it hurts *you*. Like unforgiveness and bitterness, offense is a poison that we choose to drink only hoping that the other person, our offender, will be affected. Just because we have the right to be offended doesn't mean that we should be offended. I desperately want a life that is truly free and "floats above" an offense. A life at peace with all men.

Generally, we experience offense in two stages. Stage one is actually feeling the offense. Maybe your pulse starts to rise, your emotions may rise, you may even get angry. Stage two is the choice whether or not to live offended. The resulting life impact of an offensive situation is my choice. It may sting, but the continuing pain of the sting is my choice.

Typically, when people find themselves tired, stressed, hungry/hangry, or lonely, they may be more easily offended. I love the way that Lysa Terkeurst says, "A depleted girl can quickly become a defeated girl when she lets her emotions dictate her reactions." Whenever I am living in my self-centered nature, I tend to be more easily offended which is the ultimate display of me living in the center of my smaller story. When I am walking in the "Bigger Story" of God's greater purposes, then I am not as easily offended.

The Word of God tells us that love COVERS a multitude of sin, and it is to a man's glory to overlook an offense. Scripture also reminds us that a fool is easily annoyed and that the prudent man overlooks an insult. We must not forget that each of us can inadvertently offend others as well. It goes both ways. Do I want to be the victim of the offense? Do I want to stay a victim of the offense? We choose if we want to drink the poison. Are you easily annoyed? Being unoffendable is a healthy choice and a pathway to our own peace of mind. My pastor reminds us that "our lives are too short, and our callings are too great to be offended about something small."

Ponder:

Consider how you respond to the offensive actions of others. Do you easily forgive and overlook the offense? Or do you choose to wallow around in being easily offended?

Scriptures:

Proverbs 19:11

A person's wisdom yields patience; it is to one's glory to overlook an offense.

Ephesians 4:2-3

Be completely humble and gentle; be patient, bearing with one another in love. Make every effort to keep the unity of the Spirit through the bond of peace.

Prayer:

Lord, I want you to be my defender. I need You to help me quickly release and even overlook any offense so that I may live a more peaceful life. I choose a peace-filled heart that forgives quickly. I yield my offendable heart to You.

Day 2

Perfectly Imperfect

*R*elationships can be so difficult to navigate sometimes. Taking offense starts with my response to others; and my response is my choice! Last I knew, I will be a human being until I die. I will live with humans, marry them, birth them, work with them, and have them as bosses and as neighbors. I call this our common ground: the human condition. Upon accepting Christ as Lord, we are given a new nature through the indwelling Holy Spirit. But, unfortunately, we remain living in the "human condition," often described spiritually as living in the "flesh." Since our enemy wants to kill, steal, and destroy all relationships, it is easy to understand struggles with offense caused by people ... even people we love.

If we are on a continuous search to be offended, then we will always find reasons for such. Being easily offended or irritated leads to poor responses stemming from our self-nature. We all want love, acceptance, worth, and security, but those things can only be truly fulfilled by Christ within. We live fully when we live from our new identity in Christ.

The main reason people live offended is unfulfilled expectations, whether they are unspoken, unmet, or even unrealistic. We are often offended when others don't behave like we want them to. Each human is intentionally designed to be different. We are all designed perfectly imperfect. We have different personalities, viewpoints, and experiences all leading to different rationales and behaviors. Even my children, growing up in the same home, live with completely different personalities and viewpoints.

It is easy to see another person acting like a brat, but it is not easy to see it when we behave like a brat. It is easy to see when others are irritable, easily offended, or even blamers. Yet so often we don't see that we have it within ourselves to behave the exact same way. We can see the splinter in another person's eye, yet we cannot see the log in our own. With an unoffendable heart, one chooses to quickly forgive and release the offense. God doesn't ask you to forgive to heal the other person. God asks you to forgive to heal *you*. This quick forgiveness sets you free from the burden that comes with an easily offendable heart.

It is a shame for one sinner to throw a stone at another sinner. We all live from an inborn sin nature, which is a bit messy. We all need grace and mercy for those days that we are not our best. We don't need to be provoked by offenses that can bind any of us. We don't need to live defensively either. Life is full of adventure with other perfectly imperfect humans. Let's extend lots of grace as we are all navigating the human condition.

Ponder:

How are you responding to other humans when they act differently than you think they should? Are there scenarios where you easily take offense? Do you throw stones at the poor behaviors of others? Do you ever behave poorly?

Scriptures:

Ecclesiastes 7:21-22(ESV)

Do not take to heart all the things that people say, lest you hear your servant cursing you. Your heart knows that many times you yourself have cursed others.

Ephesians 4:32

Be kind and compassionate to one another, forgiving each other, just as in Christ God forgave you.

Prayer:

Lord, I want to forgive quickly even when people "know not what they are doing" …or even if they DO know what they are doing! I need you to be my refuge and strength in times when I jump to an offendable heart. I am perfectly imperfect just like them. I yield my offendable heart to You.

Day 3

Giving Grace

*Y*ears ago, I made a decision to give others the benefit of the doubt, to believe the best in them before assuming the worst. That decision brings a lot of freedom to relationships. It was a choice to wrap my heart around the child-like faith that people aren't trying to behave poorly, trying to get it wrong, or making stupid mistakes on purpose. Here are some definitions for "benefit of the doubt":

1) The state of accepting something/someone as honest or deserving of trust even though there are doubts.

2) To default to a belief that another person's intentions are honest, and not assume malice when there is uncertainty or doubt surrounding the circumstances.

3) To decide that you will believe someone, even though you are not sure that what the person is saying is true.

4) The withholding of judgment so as to retain a favorable or at least neutral opinion of someone or something when the full information about the subject is not yet available.

5) A favorable judgment granted in the absence of full evidence.

I might behave poorly but I never intentionally choose poor behavior. Why would I assume that of others? When you give people the benefit of the doubt it allows you to believe the best in others and it brings out the best in yourself. Any of us can have bad days that can lead to bad moments. Life is not perfect, and none of us are either.

Giving people the benefit of the doubt can help offset our offendable hearts. It takes us out of the center of our small story and everything being about us. It is a way that we can honor others, even when they may not deserve it. I am simply giving away the gift of grace that God has given to me. And we cannot outgive the Gift-Giver. Do I really think that a friend running late, someone cancelling plans, my husband not emptying the dishwasher, or another spouting a short, hurtful comment or having a bad moment is really some plan against me? The truth is that all of their behaviors are for reasons other than me. It isn't a plot to irritate my heart.

If we are to obey the Lord and love the way that scripture tells us to, then we are to never give up hope that we are all learning and becoming better. The Lord loves us unconditionally and is so patient with us. He sees our sinful nature and still chooses to extend us grace and new mercies every morning. Don't you think it's time we gave each other a break and cut each other some slack? Imagine the peace if we all started extending the benefit of the doubt. Our offendable heart is a tool of the enemy to rob us of better, more fulfilling relationships. Let go of the offense!

Ponder:

Do I allow the poor behavior of others to produce an offensive, poor response from me? Am I reactive? Maybe I should consider if they are having a bad day and quickly extend grace.

Scriptures:

1 Corinthians 13:7 (ESV)

Love bears all things, believes all things, hopes all things, endures all things.

Romans 12:10 (NIV)

Be devoted to one another in love. Honor one another above yourselves.

Prayer:

Lord, help me honor others with the same patience and love that You have so generously given to me. Help me give others the benefit of the doubt as I am not to judge their behavior. I can behave poorly myself. Help me give grace! I yield my offendable heart to You.

Day 4

Vantage Points

*I*f you remember the movie "Vantage Point" from 2008, you'll be familiar with the concept that we can't assume to know reasons for other people's actions. In the movie, during an historic counter-terrorism summit in Spain, the president of the United States is struck down by an assassin's bullet. Eight strangers have a perfect view of the kill, but what did they really see? This movie portrays the story from the "vantage point" of each eye witness. Although each story has similar components, they differ from their "point of view." This movie depicts how life can easily be seen from many points of view.

There are many things out of our control. Such as who are our parents, what nation or decade we are born into, what our skin color is, etc. We all have a mother and a father. We all have a story. We all have unique personal experiences, strengths, weaknesses, personalities, core values, etc. So, our perspective can be wildly different from one another. In *The 7 Habits of Highly Effective People* by Stephen Covey, the fifth habit is, "Seek first to understand, then to be understood." Empathetic listening to others compels them to reciprocate that listening model. This leads to greater understanding and communication. It is easier to give grace to others when we understand their point of view, whether we agree with it or not.

The other day, I was standing behind a lady in the Walmart line who was so angry about not being able to find her credit card she took it out on me as well as the cashier. Her cuss words made the cashier super responsive and angry (an easily offendable heart). Her cuss words to me made me wonder what her background story had been, what had been troubling her that day, and what else was going on inside of her. I wanted to give her a big hug. I felt so sorry for her as I understood her frustration and embarrassment. But that was no reason for offense. I sought to understand her predicament. I was grateful for my journey with an unoffendable heart.

God is the only one with a pure and true vantage point. He has an eternal vantage point! We cannot know the heart of another. We probably don't know their story or the pains that drive their behaviors. But we can be slow to anger and quick to forgive even when we don't understand. We can live from a heart of compassion versus a heart that simply chooses offense.

May we all consider the vantage point that we are all a work in progress, that we all need love, grace, and mercy from others. Let it start with me.

Ponder:

Consider the fact that an irritating person might be so because of something in their background that you don't understand. Consider that others are a work-in-progress just like you. Consider that they may see things differently than you.

Scriptures:

Proverbs 18:2 (NIV)

Fools find no pleasure in understanding but delight in airing their own opinions.

James 1:19

My dear brothers and sisters, take note of this: Everyone should be quick to listen, slow to speak and slow to become angry.

Prayer:

Lord, help me seek first to understand before being understood. Help me to see through Your eyes of mercy, grace, and patient love. Help me accept another's point of view as different than mine. I yield my offendable heart to You.

Day 5

Why Am I Irritable?

A short time into my new marriage, I found myself irritated by something my husband had done "incorrectly." At least in my opinion. I may have even rolled my eyes. I was irritated. My husband responded, "Wow! After twenty-eight years, I am so glad that you finally told me that I was doing it wrong." I was humiliated at my behavior. There is more than one way to cut the apple. I was easily irritated by behaviors of others that did not match up to my expectations. What small thinking that the world should revolve around my opinion of what was "right" and how it SHOULD be done. What arrogance!

What do people do that makes you feel irritated? How about bad drivers or rude people? Does your response cause you to feel offended as well as irritated? How could you think differently to help you feel differently? Could you extend mercy wrapped in patience? Have you ever been rude? If I am offended or irritated, that is my chosen response, and that is on me. The behavior of others can't be responsible for my reaction. What you feel and how you respond is based on what you think!

After being completely irritated by the behavior of my teenagers, my husband asked, "If they are always irritating *you,* then why are *you* so irritable?" I was stunned by this question. I felt so immature. They were sucking me into their issues, and I was buying it. When we complain about the behavior of others, it reveals our offendable heart. If I had chosen to focus on all that was praiseworthy about my children, about the blessings that they are, then just maybe I would be able to navigate those years a bit differently. They were hormonal and certainly needed some grace. My constant irritation with them gave me pause to consider my maturity, my behavior, and my responses. I double-timed my prayers for grace, patience, and understanding.

An oyster takes what was at first an irritation and intrusion—a grain of sand—and uses it to enrich its value. With time, a beautiful pearl is formed. How can we reframe the irritants of life to allow growth, harvest beauty, and gain wisdom? We have to be willing to open our eyes and our hearts to see the opportunity for growth presented with every irritation. Can my irritant really be my blessing to a greater personal maturity and positivity? Maybe my irritant can smooth me out just as the sand grain smoothed the pearl into a thing of beauty and value.

Since testing produces strength and perseverance (James 1:2-4), let the transforming work begin. Ask God to give you new eyes to see and a new strength to become the great pearl resulting from life's irritations. And remember, "your life is too short and your calling too great to spend time offended." Forgive, let go, and move on to the greater glory at hand.

Ponder:

Am I easily irritated by others? Am I quick to give grace and forgiveness? What does it say about me when I am so easily irritated? I am the common denominator to all of my irritations.

Scriptures:

Philippians 2:3-4

Do nothing out of selfish ambition or vain conceit. Rather, in humility value others above yourselves, not looking to your own interests but each of you to the interests of the others.

Hebrews 12:14

Make every effort to live in peace with everyone and to be holy; without holiness no one will see the Lord.

Prayer:

Lord, forgive me for being quick to judge another. Help my love to be long-suffering, patient, kind, and full of grace. Help me not be so irritable and responsive. I yield my irritated and offendable heart to You.

CHAPTER 2

The Lie of Not Enough

*A*m I smart enough? Skinny enough? Talented enough? Patient enough? Good enough wife or mom? Am I enough?

These were the questions that came to mind when, in 2013, I was writing my book *Are You Enough?* and my book coach asked me, "If this book could answer one question, what would it be?" I pondered. What was one of the greatest questions in my heart and the heart of my potential readers? I replied that most people, especially women, struggle with wondering if we have what it takes. I know I have. Maybe you're like me. If so, this chapter is for you.

We all question our capabilities at one time or another. Do we have what it takes for whatever assignment is at hand? It could be a job, a marriage, a class, or a new relationship.

Questioning my own sufficiency increased with marriage. If you're married, you might know what I mean! Could I make it until "death do us part?" Then the uncertainty increased with parenting. It peaked when I considered homeschooling our four children. We all ask similar questions, "Do I actually have what it takes to _____?" (You fill in the blank).

When I was a teen and young adult, I walked in all sorts of crazy confidence of doing it bigger and better than my parents, my teachers, and my world. That confidence must have stemmed from my inexperience and immaturity. I was so confident and yet so naïve. This confidence was certainly untested. It was filled with hope but not filled with years of wisdom. We all need the dreams of those youth-filled days. We are inspired by such. We just need to add the wisdom of the years as well. Alas, the dilemma. This was my question of "enoughness." Is that even a word? It is now!

We all need to settle this question of sufficiency or forever live under the yoke and illusion of the never measuring up to the load. I was overwhelmed with the doubt of sufficiency. I needed more freedom to navigate my days. So, what did God have in mind when He created me and assigned me good works for the days of my life? He is my Creator and my Knower. Scripture says that He equips those that He calls. Teach me, Lord.

Ponder:

In what areas do you feel inadequate to handle the job at hand? Does the "whatever you need to be enough" line keep moving farther and farther away?

Scriptures:

Hebrews 13:20-21

Now may the God of peace [...] equip you with everything good for doing His will, and may He work in us what is pleasing to Him, through Jesus Christ, to whom be glory for ever and ever. Amen.

Philippians 4:19

And my God will meet all your needs according to the riches of His glory in Christ Jesus.

Prayer:

Lord, I don't question Your design but I do question my sufficiency. Teach me the wisdom to work from Your strength in Your assignments. Help me to rest in the sufficiency of your design. I yield the lie of not enough to You.

Day 2
The Void Within

W e were all created with a God-shaped VOID in our hearts – an innate longing for something more, something transcendent, something "other." This was not accidental but intentional. If we can understand this concept, we can understand our wanderings as well as our empty hearts. Ecclesiastes 3:11 refers to God's placing of "eternity in man's heart." But in this world, we often try to fill that heart-longing with material possessions, with a marriage, with children, with good intentions, or with some kind of illusive "success." Some try to fill these "voids" with the lesser things including drugs, alcohol, medications, and poor relationships. The enemy of your soul never wants you to understand the truth about your heart's God-shaped void. He is the great deceiver and comes only to rob, kill, and destroy.

The Lord created us to live in a relationship with Him in order to fill that spiritual "God-shaped" void in our hearts. He is the answer and completion to our longing hearts. But God also created us with the gift of choice. He wanted us to CHOOSE a relationship with Him, our Creator, the Knitter, the Designer, and the Knower! He knocks at the door of our hearts. He beckons us through nature, right relationships, and His Word. Only God can show us our true worth. If we believe our worth is tied to anything but God, then those things will take God's place in our life. Anything but a right relationship with Him will leave us falling short with this ongoing void within.

His Word is the owner's manual for our empty hearts and successful living. Our completeness is found in relationship with Him. Nothing will satisfy that God-shaped void in our hearts that only He was designed to fulfill. The void within is a gift to draw us to Him for the fulfillment of our souls. Choose how you fill this void carefully. Your life truly depends on it.

As long as you look to this world to validate you, there will be an emptiness in your heart. There is a God-shaped void in all our hearts, and only He can fill it.

Ponder:

How can you become more aware of your attempts to fill your heart's void with other things besides the intended relationship with your Creator and Designer?

Scripture:

Ecclesiastes 3:11

He has made everything beautiful in its time. He has also set eternity in the human heart; yet no one can fathom what God has done from beginning to end.

2 Peter 1:3

His divine power has given us everything we need for a godly life through our knowledge of Him who called us by His own glory and goodness.

Prayer:

Lord, thank you for designing me with a God-shaped void that draws me to a relationship with You like a thirsty soul is drawn to water. Teach me to live satisfied in You alone. I yield the lie of not enough to You.

Day 3

The Gift of Sufficiency

Sufficiency is a gift of grace. Do we REALLY want to be in charge of the world? Or do we just want to do what we want to do and do it truly well? Our personal control freak acts as if we actually want to be in control. This is common. It is simply the pride of man. We want to be wise with the gifts we've been given. Scripture says that many are the plans of a man, but it is the Lord's purposes that prevail. I desire the Lord's greater purposes to prevail. I am only capable of accomplishing what I could hope, imagine, or envision. But what if God's plans offer so much MORE than we could ever hope or imagine? We don't even know how to fathom this. The true journey is in letting go of our "less" in exchange for His "more."

So, if you were offered "His will, His way" or "Your will, your way," the choice would seem obvious. But the devil is sly and sneaky. He disguises good as evil and evil as good. Praise God that what the enemy intends for evil, God can turn for our good. So the question of sufficiency or "enoughness" relates to a question of, "Who is really driving this car? This life?"

God doesn't call us to run the world. But He does call us to follow Him and trust Him. "And God is able to make all grace abound to you, so that having all sufficiency in all things at all times, you may abound in every good work" (2 Corinthians 9:8 ESV). Sufficiency is a gift that allows us to abound in every good work for all the things to which we are gifted and called. God knew that we could not do it on our own. He never wanted us to. He wants us to live in the fulfillment of His greater plans and purposes for our lives. He has equipped us for the "good works" that He has called us to do.

We don't want to waste our time doing those things that we are NOT called to do. But we can do all the things that God has called us to. Do we live outside the boundaries of His calling and carry a burden that is too great? Let's lean into the voice of the Shepherd. Let's accept His gift of sufficiency and unload ourselves otherwise.

Ponder:

Ponder the thought that you are strong enough and capable enough to do whatever God has called you to do. How can you walk in the truth that His sufficiency is a gift?

Scriptures:

1 Peter 5:8

Be alert and of sober mind. Your enemy the devil prowls around like a roaring lion looking for someone to devour.

2 Corinthians 9:8

And God is able to bless you abundantly, so that in all things at all times, having all that you need, you will abound in every good work.

Prayer:

Lord, I want to abound in every good work that You have assigned me. Help me get out of the driver's seat of my life. Do not let me get in the way of Your greater purposes for my life. I yield the lie of not enough to You.

Day 4

When Less is More and More is Less

$\mathcal{H}$ow do we end up overloaded and overwhelmed? I was just speaking at a ladie's event called "Encouragement by Chocolate." Yes! What an ingenious name. The topic was "When More is Less." The Lord does equip us with what we need for our journey. Though, as a traveler through this life, we often decide, so to speak, to place more in our "backpack" than He calls us to carry. He never asked us to handle all the cares of the world or all the cares of our family on our shoulders. He never invited our control freak to grip our people or our plans. May I remind you that He actually teaches that many are the PLANS in a man's heart, but it is the Lord's purpose that prevails. Why in the world do we set out to load our lives, our backpacks, with more than He planned for us to carry? This seems like a maneuver in insanity! Why would we do such a thing? Do we feel like this would make us more important? What an illusion. This yoke is too heavy. I have learned that "MORE" often leads to much "LESS."

The load of "MORE" is a weight I no longer choose to carry. I just can't. My sanity depends on wisdom in this area. My family's health and well-being teeters on my decisions to not take on more than I am assigned. So today I want to challenge you to consider that He equips you with all you NEED to live out the life that He has called you to. You have unique giftings to use to bless others. We are not to carry the load of more than we are called to. Consider and be very selective in your "YESes." Do many of them need to become "NOs"? Pray for wisdom in each choice. Remember that each YES is a NO to other things.

Don't let the stress of your "yes" bring about too much overload. He will lead, guide, and direct our steps as we yield to His ways. What do you need to unload from your backpack? Let go and live in the freedom of less because less often leads to a life of more. More peace. More rest.

Ponder:

How are you contributing to your own overload and overwhelm? What steps can you take to be super selective in your "yeses?" What can you delegate?

Scriptures:

Proverbs 19:21

Many are the plans in a person's heart, but it is the Lord's purpose that prevails.

Luke 12:15

Then He said to them, "Watch out! Be on your guard against all kinds of greed; life does not consist in an abundance of possessions."

Prayer:

Lord, forgive me for packing too much into the journey of my life. The load is too heavy, and I have no one to blame. Help me take on Your yoke and have the wisdom to make wiser choices. Help me navigate better "yeses" and have the courage to say "no" when needed. I need to walk in Your peace. I yield the lie of not enough to You.

Day 5
All of Him, in All of Me

*T*he book *The Indwelling Life of Christ*, by Major W. Ian Thomas, has a subtitle *All of Him, In All of Me*. Major Thomas invited me to consider the importance of daily dying, to myself and my control freak ideas, in order to really live. So, what is REALLY LIVING? I pursued the thought of intentional living in my original design. This led me to crave His will, His way instead of my will, my way. This pursuit of daily dying to myself and living His will, His way has introduced me to a deeply satisfying freedom. This is where our true sufficiency is established.

My sufficiency for this life will never come from my brains, my college degree, my skills, or my personal assets. The Christian life is not about our own capacity or our own abilities. It is about God's access to fulfilling His will for our days. The only true limit to my adequacy is my availability. It's not about who we are, but about who He is. It's not about what we offer, but about what He offers us, which is all of Himself and His power working through our empty and yielded selves. The key to my sufficiency is my dependency. My control freak personality doesn't like this at all. It doesn't make earthly sense. But the wisdom of the years has taught me the power-filled truth of this concept: a "dying to live" so to speak.

Now my prayer is for all of Him to be in all of me for all of my days. Less of me, more of Him. That is my hope! I ask the Lord to help me get myself out of His way, out of the driver's seat of my own life. He can do so much more through my empty self than I could accomplish through lots of toil and labor. Since He is the vine and I am a branch, I know that whenever my "vine" is totally plugged into His "branch" that He will produce His fruit through me and not of my own effort but by His power. Not by my strength, nor by my might but by the Spirit of the Lord. I need ALL of Him in ALL of me, ALL the time. This is true freedom.

Ponder:

How could I spend more of my time inviting the Holy Spirit to lead, guide, and direct my days? Ponder the thought that His will, His way would be better than my will, my way.

Scriptures:

John 3:30

He must become greater; I must become less.

Galatians 2:20

I have been crucified with Christ and I no longer live, but Christ lives in me. The life I now live in the body, I live by faith in the Son of God, who loved me and gave Himself for me.

Prayer:

Oh Lord, please forgive me for being such a control freak and centering myself in the very middle of my world. Teach me the wisdom of daily dying so that I can truly live. I want all of You in all of me! Always. I yield the lie of not enough to You.

*I*s there ever a time where we could have more than enough? There is a Bible story about the need to feed a large, hungry crowd. It aligns with my feelings of needing to feed my husband, my family, or my people with the important things of life, liberty, and happiness. As the story goes, a young boy had two fish and five loaves in his lunch, which was not enough to feed the hungry crowd. The question of sufficiency arose! There were doubters in the crowd. I have been a doubter in the crowd. I can relate to this story! I didn't have two fish or five loaves in my lunchbox, but I did only have my personality, my giftings, my family heritage, my past, my strengths, and my weaknesses to offer to others.

In the hands of the boy, the lunch would never feed the crowd. But when ALL of his lunch was given to Jesus the Multiplier, then, not only was the crowd fed, but there were twelve baskets left over. How can this be? Was it a miracle? Absolutely! The Multiplier multiplies when He has the food and sees the need. The boy had to surrender and give Him everything first though.

This story taught me that whenever I keep my gifts, my talents, and my strengths under my control and authority, it will not be enough. However, when I give ALL that I have and ALL that I am to the Giver Himself. He multiplies it to be more than enough. I have the responsibility to give back and yield. He has the responsibility to produce the results. All I have to do is all that I can do, and I have to trust God to do that which I cannot do. Goodness! This is so mind blowing for my control freak nature to understand. That is why He said to "lean not on my own understanding" (Proverbs 3:5). You are not in charge of "feeding the whole crowd of 5000," (Matthew 14:17) or whatever your burden seems to be. You are in charge of living a yielded life and returning everything He has blessed you with so that it can be multiplied. This is a hard concept but, certainly, a freeing one. We are to work heartily, as unto the Lord, for sure. But we can trust the results to a faithful, trustworthy Abba Father. Even when we don't understand.

It is HE that makes you enough! Through His call, His strength, His provision. You were never designed to feed the 5000, the "others" of your life. He designed you with a need for Him to multiply your efforts to be "more than enough," just like the fish and the loaves. Give Him your all so that He can do the multiplying!

Ponder:

What ways can you offer your strengths and your gifts back unto the Lord for His multiplying use? Are you hanging on to the insufficiency of your own lunch?

Scriptures:

Matthew 14:17-20

"We have here only five loaves of bread and two fish," they answered. "Bring them here to me," He said. And He directed the people to sit down on the grass. Taking the five loaves and the two fish and looking up to heaven, He gave thanks and broke the loaves. Then He gave them to the disciples, and the disciples gave them to the people. They all ate and were satisfied, and the disciples picked up twelve basketfuls of broken pieces that were left over. The number of those who ate was about 5,000 men, besides women and children.

Psalm 9:10

Those who know Your name trust in You, for You, Lord, have never forsaken those who seek You.

Prayer:

Dear Lord, please take all of my "lunchbox" everything that I have. I give everything, every person, every goal, every dream, every load that I have – to You. I trust You to multiply it to be more than enough. Thank You for being trustworthy Lord. I yield the lie of not enough to You.

CHAPTER 3

The Grateful Heart

*C*an you live with deep down joy even when you don't feel it?

Years ago, I remember suffocating in a season of heartbreak and discouragement. We were massively broke, my teens were rebellious and lying, and my parents were dying. Depression was knocking at my door. During this challenging time, I was invited to open my eyes to the awe and the gifts all around me even amidst my darkness. I was encouraged to open my eyes to "all that was praiseworthy" as a new way of SEEING. There are always gifts sprinkled throughout our pain. What if I could be full of joy even when my circumstances were harsh and difficult?

Day 1

Joy and Happiness

*M*ost people are confused with the distinction between joy and happiness, but the difference is substantial. Most people seek happiness as a life goal, but deep, satisfying joy is the real prize. Often, we move through our days performing one tedious task after another—washing clothes, cooking dinner, and catering to a demanding boss without much joy or happiness. The truth is the Bible never promises happiness; however, it does promise joy. It even says our joy may be *full* or *complete…* a better goal.

Happiness is an emotion based upon *happenings*. It's easy to be happy when things are going well … when you have freedom from suffering, financial security, and all your relationships are good. But when you have trouble with one or more of these areas in life, what happens to your "happiness?" It's probably gone. And you feel sad.

On the other hand, joy is a stronger, deeper, yet less common feeling than happiness. It is not dependent on circumstances. It is rooted in who God is. It is birthed out of relationship with God as "In His presence is the fullness of joy. At His right hand are pleasures forevermore" (Psalm 16:11). His joy supernaturally sustains our souls in seasons of heartache, injustice, and sorrow. Enduring the valleys of life is nearly impossible without the life-giving fuel of joy in Christ.

Pastor Rick Warren is quoted as saying, "Joy is the settled assurance that God is in control of all the details of my life, the quiet confidence that ultimately everything is going to be alright, and the determined choice to praise God in every situation." Let's settle our hearts in this assurance and hope.

Joy can also be a by-product grounded in the idea of doing something good for someone. We have joy when—even in our suffering—we are acting for the benefit of someone else's well-being. If you have ever selflessly given of yourself or your possessions, you are certainly familiar with this feeling of joy.

Simply, happiness is a feeling, joy is a choice. Happiness is what you get from the world and so it's dependent on your circumstances, but joy is what you pour into the world from your own heart, and all it requires is for you to open the flood gates. Choosing to seek and find the blessings sprinkled throughout our pain will help our anxious heart give way to a powerful, new, grateful heart.

So, what motivates us in life? Is it the pursuit of happiness, or an overflow of joy? If all of our efforts are focused on trying to be happy, we are missing the point. But if our purpose is to have joy in a fulfilling life, then we have to commit to the Lord and love one another in a way that seeks something better than just personal self-satisfaction.

What are you doing in your world that is causing you joy? Are you connecting with God and others through relationship and service? Do something good for someone else—and see how you feel. This is joy. Paul tells us if we walk in the ways of God, joy is a resulting fruit of the Spirit. So also is love, peace, patience, kindness, goodness, faithfulness, gentleness, and self-control.

Having joy includes feeling happy. But being happy doesn't always include joy. May the joy of the Lord be your strength.

Ponder:

Ponder the difference between your happiness based on happenings and your joy based on an inexhaustible relationship with your heavenly Father. How could you increase your security and trust? Tether your heart to His faithful character and His gift of joy.

Scripture:

John 15:11

I have told you this so that My joy may be in you and that your joy may be complete.

Romans 15:13

May the God of hope fill you with all joy and peace as you trust in Him, so that you may overflow with hope by the power of the Holy Spirit.

Prayer:

Lord, help me recognize the difference between worldly happiness and Your gift of deep abiding joy. Continue to develop this fruit of Your Spirit within me. Every day I choose a grateful heart.

Day 2

My Journal of Gratitude

*D*epression and anxiety are suffocating emotions. During a particularly difficult season in my life, I fought back the onslaught of both. To name a few of the issues: My teens were lying, my parents were dying, we were dog broke, and I was dealing with too many menopausal issues to count. I was spinning plates as fast as I could and yet there was no peace on the horizon. Life felt extremely heavy! The burdens I carried were weighing me down into a miserable pit. But as a Christian, I even piled shame on myself for feeling this way. Wasn't I supposed to be living an abundant life? BUT GOD! He graciously intervened.

During that particularly difficult season, I read the book *1000 Gifts* by Anne Voskamp. Desperately needing some oxygen for living, and inspired by Anne's story, I started journaling everything that I could possibly be grateful for. I asked God to open my eyes to even the smallest gift ... like a knuckle to help wrap my finger around my coffee cup, like heating and air conditioning, like toilet paper, like fresh air. This daily exercise didn't lift me out of my pit immediately, but it started a rich journey toward a new type of wholeness, a wholeness birthed through the lens of a grateful heart. As I continue to diligently open my eyes and my heart to all the gifts in my life, I began to recognize them *everywhere*. It was like there was a whole new world to appreciate that I hadn't taken the time to see or made the choice to notice.

Across weeks of writing down and "naming" these gifts, a light-heartedness developed even amidst the trials of each day. My grateful heart slowly pushed out the weightiness of my days. I began to realize that a grateful heart and an anxious heart could not simultaneously reside in the same person at the same time. It was either anxiety or gratitude taking up the space of my heart. I became excited to venture into each new day with *new eyes* to see *new gifts*. Depression gave way to gratitude and gratitude became my best antidepressant. Not just a "one and done" type gratitude, but a consistent, diligent gratitude that almost refused to be sucked back into that pit of despair again. My life was too precious to live that way.

I flew through my list of 1000 gifts within months and decided that this was a new way of life. A grateful heart had transformed my days. Even more exciting, my grateful heart began to permeate my home and my family. So many things began to change when I changed my "SEEING" and my heart. This is a battleground worth fighting on. I celebrated this new life-giving habit. I've learned to be a gold miner for those things in life that are praiseworthy in order to continue to thrive from a grateful heart.

Ponder:

Ponder the tension between your gratitude and depression, between joy and sadness. How can you make deliberate choices to open your eyes and journal all the gifts you have been given?

Scripture:

1 Thessalonians 5:18

Give thanks in all circumstances; for this is God's will for you in Christ Jesus.

Ephesians 5:20

[...] always giving thanks to God the Father for everything, in the name of our Lord Jesus Christ.

Prayer:

Lord, help me constantly and daily choose to see Your gifts everywhere. Open my eyes to all my blessings. Help me to choose to give You thanks in all things as I trust Your faithfulness. Every day I choose a grateful heart.

Day 3
Developing a New Habit

Whatever we do repetitively, whether that's biting our nails or making time to exercise, slowly becomes a habit. In fact, Ninety percent of our thoughts are repetitive, so they really become a *strong habit*. If we want to develop a new habit, we have to think about the things that we think about! The thoughts on the feedback loop in our mind often come out in our words and our actions. Trash in always leads to trash out. If we think about all the junk in our lives, then complaints are likely to come out of our mouths. If we think about all the things that we are grateful for, then gratitude for life bubbles over.

Gratitude is a fierce weapon! It turns out that gratitude is highly correlated with well-being and life satisfaction. My new habit of journaling gratitude, over time, was deeply impactful to my heart and my family. This was a new, intimate, life-giving, personal habit that I could actually be in charge of myself. I decided that I never wanted to stop giving thanks. No one was responsible for my new habit of gratitude but me. This new habit was producing a change in my heart and my home.

Our enemy comes to steal, kill, and destroy our joy. Gratitude is a weapon against the enemy of our souls. Since life is hard, cultivating a grateful heart isn't always an easy task, but it is well worth the effort. Our enemy wants us to give in and give up, sinking into hopelessness, depression, and despair. But if we keep noticing the good, if we keep looking toward our divine Redeemer, then our hope will never be consumed by hopelessness. Our commitment and diligence to be grateful is a life-time game changer.

Our heart becomes even more grateful when we experience the significant love of Christ and His redeeming work in our lives. As the intimacy of our relationship with God grows, so grows our gratitude. Each day, a gift for the greater glory is at hand. The intertwining of relationship with God and gratitude is real.

The Bible tells us to give thanks in ALL things for this is the will of God for us. Really, ALL things? It helped me to realize that the Bible didn't say FOR all things but IN all things. This is a reflection of our child-like and confident trust in the Trustworthy ONE. When I choose to give thanks in all things, I choose to release the reins of my control and surrender to the One who loves me most.

Develop the habit of having a grateful heart. Wield this weapon against your enemy. It will be a game-changer for your days.

Ponder:

Ponder your thoughts and the daily activity of your heart. Is gratitude a mental habit? How can you develop this new habit of a more grateful heart?

Scripture:

Philippians 4:6

Do not be anxious about anything, but in every situation, by prayer and petition, with thanksgiving, present your requests to God.

Psalm 9:1

I will give thanks to You, Lord, with all my heart; I will tell of all Your wonderful deeds.

Prayer:

Oh Lord, I want to give thanks in all things. Help me develop the new habit of a grateful heart. Help me build new mental pathways of grateful thinking. Every day I choose a grateful heart.

Day 4

The Impact of Gratitude

*D*id you know that there is actually cognitive science behind the impact of gratitude? Most of us intuitively recognize that it is good to stop and smell the roses every once in a while, acknowledging all that we could be grateful for. But gratitude really changes the brain and body for the better! But did you also know that gratitude has a direct correlation to success? Gratitude affects our bodies biologically. It increases our longevity, our ability to use our imagination, and our ability to solve problems.

"Dr. Caroline Leaf is a communication pathologist and cognitive neuroscientist with a Masters and PhD in Communication Pathology and a BSc in Logopaedics, specializing in cognitive and metacognitive neuropsychology. Since the early 1980s she has researched the mind-brain connection, the nature of mental health, and the formation of memory. She was one of the first in her field to study how the brain can change (neuroplasticity) with directed mind input." (*Bio at DrLeaf.com*)

Dr. Leaf, along with other professionals, has recognized the impact of gratitude on our brain. If we think differently, we can live differently. The benefits of gratitude on our hearts is astounding. Here are a few scientifically proven benefits of gratitude:

1. Gratitude opens the door to more relationships. Not only does saying "thank you" constitute good manners, but showing appreciation can help you win new friends (*according to a 2014 study published in Emotion*).

2. Gratitude improves physical health. Grateful people experience fewer aches and pains and report feeling healthier than other people (*according to a 2012 study published in Personality and Individual Differences*).

3. Gratitude improves psychological health. Gratitude reduces a multitude of toxic emotions, from envy and resentment to frustration and regret. Robert Emmons, a leading gratitude researcher, confirms that gratitude effectively increases happiness and reduces depression.

4. Gratitude enhances empathy and reduces aggression. Grateful people are more likely to behave in a prosocial manner, even when others behave less kindly, according to a 2012 study by the University of Kentucky.

5. Grateful people sleep better. Writing in a gratitude journal improves sleep, according to a 2011 study published in *Applied Psychology: Health and Well-Being*.

6. Gratitude improves self-esteem. Studies have shown that gratitude reduces social comparisons. Rather than becoming resentful toward people who have more money or better jobs—a major factor in reduced self-esteem—grateful people are able to appreciate other people's accomplishments.

7. For years, research has shown gratitude not only reduces stress, but it may also play a major role in overcoming trauma. Recognizing all that you have to be thankful for—even during the worst times—fosters resilience. (www.forbes.com *7 Scientific Proven Benefits of Gratitude* [...] by Amy Morin)

We all have the ability and opportunity to cultivate gratitude. Rather than complain about the things, take a few moments to focus on all that you *have*. Research proves that developing an "attitude of gratitude" is one of the biggest game-changers to improve your satisfaction with life.

Ponder:

How can you become more aware of your levels of gratitude? Ponder the thought of gratitude enhancing your satisfaction with life.

Scripture:

2 Corinthians 4:15

All this is for your benefit, so that the grace that is reaching more and more people may cause thanksgiving to overflow to the glory of God.

1 Chronicles 16:34

Give thanks to the Lord, for He is good; His love endures forever.

Prayer:

Lord, You tell us to give thanks in all things for this is Your will for us. I want Your will. Help me to develop a deeper heart of gratitude. Every day I choose a grateful heart.

Day 5

Developing a Grateful Mindset

*J*ust like good habits, a grateful mindset will make a huge impact on your personal satisfaction with life. A mindset of gratitude increases mental strength and is registered in the brain as optimism. Thoughts are such powerful triggers and when repeated frequently, new neural pathways are formed—like well-worn highways in your brain. This happens with any type of repetitive thinking but can be harnessed for positivity with a regular gratitude practice. Frequent thoughts of gratitude train the brain to choose positive thoughts.

Consistency is the key to changing your mindset and, therefore, your life. Switching your internal chatter to thoughts of gratitude and appreciation doesn't just happen overnight. Consider adding new action steps to cultivate a grateful mindset. Here are some suggestions:

- Start a gratefulness journal. Record personal gratitude daily.

- Open your eyes to see "all that which is praiseworthy."

- Guard your heart and mind by limiting negative input.

- Express your gratitude to others.

- Share and speak about things you are grateful for with those around you.

- Ask the Holy Spirit to help you and then yield to His work.

- Interrupt anxious moments with a good praise and worship song.

- Break the habit of complaining with a grateful comment.

- Start learning to see the silver-lining in circumstances.

- Give others grace and the benefit of the doubt.

- Imagine what eternal perspective could look like to bring good out of a situation.

- Volunteer to serve the less fortunate.

- Meditate every morning and evening on what you are thankful for in your life.

- Pause when you find yourself feeling down, think about all the good things in your life.

- Read God's Word daily and with your family.

- Model and encourage a grateful heart in your home.

- Pray daily and also together with others you love.

- Model a life of thoughtfulness and sacrifice for others.

Gratitude is a mindset just like ingratitude is. A grateful heart leads us to more of everything. More satisfaction. More hope. More joy. Even better relationships. Gratitude turns what we have into enough. True gratitude is a daily choice that will impact your life for the better. Ponder these thoughts:

God is completely good. God is constantly good. God is unchangeably good. God will never not be good. God could never be less than good. Everything our God does is good. God gives you a peace that passes understanding. God gives you the Holy Spirit to convict, strengthen, and encourage. God gives you His Word as a guide. God gives you health to bless you. Friends to love you. Life to enjoy. God has never stopped being good, we have just started being grateful.

I am living proof that there is a beautiful and transforming power in a grateful heart. Won't you consider this life-changing habit?

Ponder:

Consider reasons that you are not as grateful as you might want to be. What does gratitude look like in your life? Besides the habit of gratitude, do you have a mindset of gratitude?

Scripture:

Psalm 103:2-5

Praise the Lord, my soul, and forget not all His benefits—who forgives all your sins and heals all your diseases, who redeems your life from the pit and crowns you with love and compassion, who satisfies your desires with good things so that your youth is renewed like the eagle's.

Psalm 145:1-3

I will exalt You, my God the King; I will praise Your name for ever and ever. Every day I will praise You and extol Your name for ever and ever. Great is the Lord and most worthy of praise; His greatness no one can fathom.

Prayer:

Lord, I need You and I am grateful for Your unending goodness to me. Help me develop a mindset of gratitude for all You are and have given me. I want to focus on You and all my blessings. Every day I choose a grateful heart.

CHAPTER 4

A "Dying" to Live

*H*ave you ever been trying so hard to find something—love, joy, peace, strength, whatever—but no matter how hard you try, it seems to elude you?

There seemed to have been several times in life where I felt like I was "going backwards" only to learn that it was my best path forward. I have learned to yield my perceived "rightness" in the moment to show a greater love for the relationship at hand. It felt like I was "dying" in the power struggle of the moment but ultimately it allowed a greater love to win. As a seed has to die and be sown into the ground, sometimes we have to yield and die in the moment for there to be a greater growth in the future. We have to often die to our schedule, our plans, and our people in order to thrive in our life. The grace, humility, and maturity it takes to die to ourselves so that someone else may live more deeply loved mirrors what Jesus did for you and me on the cross. These moments are difficult but so rewarding in the long run!

Dying to live—what a paradox!

Day 1

What is Biblical Paradox?

*L*et's discuss Biblical paradoxes. A paradox is defined as an apparently self-contradictory declaration but is, in fact, true. To some, biblical paradoxes may seem confusing, a bit absurd, and even somewhat ridiculous. Yet these very words of God were written for our admonition and learning. Wrapping our minds around their truths can bring a freedom unbeknownst to this world. Praise God that His Word reminds us to "lean not on our own understanding but to acknowledge Him and He will make the paths straight" (Proverbs 3:5-6). This takes faith. This takes trust. This brings freedom.

Today, let's consider a few counter-intuitive principles:

1. EXALTATION THROUGH HUMILITY (James 4:10)
   God has never been pleased with the proud, boastful, and over-confident. He created us for His ultimate purposes and glory, not for our own. He delights in a humble spirit. It takes real wisdom and strength to walk in true humility.

2. STRENGTH THROUGH WEAKNESS (2 Cor. 12:10)
   With all our God-given privileges and advantages; there is always the possibility of being overconfident in our own strength. God often allows a "thorn in the flesh" to keep us ever dependent on Him, so that we can walk in our ultimate strength. Can we see this as a gift?

3. RECEIVING THROUGH GIVING (Acts 20:35)
   Giving can seem quite foolish to selfish people. Some of the most miserable people on earth are those who take and take. Some of the happiest people are givers for they manifest and reflect God in their unselfish attitude. They become His channel of blessing! When we cheerfully and willingly give our time, talent, or treasure for God's glory, in return, we receive love, joy, peace, satisfaction, and respect from men!

4. GAINING THROUGH LOSING (Phil. 3:7-8)
Materialism, fame, and love of money have always been the greatest hindrances to a personal living relationship with the Lord. You can gain the whole world but lose your own soul (Mark 8:36), or like Paul you can lose earthly opportunities but gain Christ and lay-up treasure in heaven!

5. LIVING THROUGH DYING (John 12:24)
The kernel of wheat that falls to the ground and dies also grows and becomes productive. This is an agricultural and a spiritual principle as well. Death to the old self is the first step to Christian growth. The more you die to SELF, the more CHRIST is seen in you! John the Baptist said that Christ must increase, and we must decrese (John 3:30).

Ponder:

How can you consider each of these paradoxes and apply them to your life in a more significant way? Pray for a greater understanding of these truths.

Scriptures:

John 12:24

Very truly I tell you, unless a kernel of wheat falls to the ground and dies, it remains only a single seed. But if it dies, it produces many seeds.

2 Corinthians 12:10

That is why, for Christ's sake, I delight in weaknesses, in insults, in hardships, in persecutions, in difficulties. For when I am weak, then I am strong.

Prayer:

Lord, teach me the power of living Your great paradoxical mysteries. I want to live in the freedom that You offer through living in Your ways. Help me to lean not on my own understanding but to trust in You alone. I want to "die" to myself in order to really live for You.

Day 2

Created for Purpose

*C*reators create things with reason, purpose, and intention. Things don't just accidentally appear. Scriptures say that we were knit together ... fearfully and wonderfully ... in the secret place ... with days assigned to each of us. That doesn't sound accidental. It goes on to say that we were knit as the Creator's "masterpiece/handiwork [...] to do good works, which God prepared in advance for us to do" (Ephesians 2:10). Whoa! So, I was planned ON purpose, WITH purpose, and FOR purpose? He intentionally created me, gifted me, and has a personalized calling on my life.

When I was little, much like you, I had big dreams of what life would be like when I grew up. I had plans. Big plans. My will, my way so to speak. But, somehow, my entire world didn't cooperate with all my "big plans." As years and experience bred greater learning and wisdom, I realized that I am not completely in charge of my world. I needed the cooperation of other humans. I had a hope to do things the "right way." But what was that? My spouse had one opinion. My boss had another opinion. My children had another opinion. All about the right way. After a season of heart-breaking life lessons, I read about the grace of yielding. We have a choice of yielding to others, but I pondered the idea of yielding to God's greater plans and purposes for my life, not just my little girl dreams. I was reminded of Jesus' words and His example: "My Father, if it is possible, may this cup be taken from me. Yet not as I will, but as you will" (Matthew 26:39). This statement shows the yielding or the dying of self. Jesus chose the will of the Father over his own will. This highlights a definite "dying of self to live to greater purposes."

We are all self-centered creatures with a vast propensity for selfishness and "my will, my way." Consider the grace of yielding to "His will, His way." As our creator, His original ways for our lives are higher than ours as His thoughts and plans are higher than ours. When you die to your self-centered ways, you then discover the beauty and power within yourself that God intended—Christ in you, the hope of glory. We live in the greatest fullness of life when we are in the sweet center of that purpose and that plan. Consider this dying to live.

Ponder:

How can you live a life with a grace to yield to God's greater plans and purposes for your days? Ponder your life's story for His greater glory. It will likely be different than you think.

Scriptures:

Psalm 139:13-16

For You created my inmost being; You knit me together in my mother's womb. I praise You because I am fearfully and wonderfully made; Your works are wonderful, I know that full well. My frame was not hidden from You when I was made in the secret place, when I was woven together in the depths of the earth. Your eyes saw my unformed body; all the days ordained for me were written in Your book before one of them came to be.

Isaiah 55:8-9

"For My thoughts are not your thoughts, neither are your ways My ways," declares the *Lord*. "As the heavens are higher than the earth, so are My ways higher than your ways and My thoughts than your thoughts."

Prayer:

Oh Lord! I need Your help to remind me that I truly do want "Your will, Your way" over "my will, my way" as Your ways are so much higher than I could think, hope, or imagine. I choose to die to myself and my ways so that I can live for Your greater purposes for my life. Lead, guide, and direct my steps! I want to "die" to myself in order to really live for You.

Day 3

A Paradigm Shift

A paradigm is a person's frame of reference. Their paradigm is how they see the world based on all the information that they have gathered and the beliefs that they possess. A "paradigm shift" occurs when our usual way of thinking about or doing something is replaced by a new and different way thinking or acting. Paradigm shifts often occur around what we call "AHA moments" when we suddenly understand something in a new or different way allowing us to see the world in a new light.

As we venture through our teenage years and mature into young adults, most of us start recognizing that we have a paradigm of control within us. I refer to this as our inner "control freak." It is sometimes dominant, sometimes abated. In this paradigm, we often think that we are the center of our world. That we are in charge and that everything will go according to our plans. As time and age bring wisdom, we learn that we cannot control other people or circumstances. However, it is imperative to know that we can control our responses.

The response of "letting go of control and letting God" have His way in our lives is a choice to unload the pressure of outcomes. Through faith, yielding ultimate control of the "uncontrollable things" leads to a peace of mind that brings rest. This is dying to live. The burden is shifted. As we walk yielded to His higher purposes, life will become a more beautiful journey. Our control-freak often leads us down a road full of resentment, exhaustion, disbelief, and disappointment.

Don't get me wrong. Life is full of choices that we do control. We can control the temperature in our house, decide what we are going to eat for dinner, etc. But there is so much beyond our control like the weather, others' behaviors, the news, and many circumstances. We do have the personal responsibility to do all that we can do, but then to trust God with that which we cannot do. Everything in this universe belongs to the Lord. He is actually in control of all things. He even gives humans choice. He will bring glory to His children, He will protect His children, He will carry the burdens of His children. In Him, all things hold together. I am grateful that I am not in charge of the world and I can find rest in that. Our surrender is first an event and then it becomes a way that we choose to live. Someday, we will need to make a paradigm shift from wanting control to wanting the rest that comes from trusting He is in control. Is today that day?

Ponder:

How can you die to your inner control freak and choose to walk in a greater trust in our *Good Good Father*? How can you walk in more of the peace that He offers?

Scriptures:

Proverbs 19:21

Many are the plans in a person's heart, but it is the *Lord*'s purpose that prevails.

Colossians 1:16-17

For in Him all things were created: things in heaven and on earth, visible and invisible, whether thrones or powers or rulers or authorities; all things have been created through Him and for Him. He is before all things, and in Him all things hold together.

Prayer:

Lord, I am so exhausted by trying to be in charge of my entire world. Teach me Your ways and give me the grace to yield to Your greater plans for my life. Help me shift my paradigm from desiring control to yielding control. I want to "die" to myself in order to really live for You.

Day 4

Fear and Faith

"*Fear* not!" is the most repeated command in the Bible. In fact, Lloyd Ogilvie in *Facing the Future without Fear* even said there are 366 "fear nots" in the Bible, one for every day of the year, including Leap Year! God doesn't want us to go a single day without hearing His encouragement and word of comfort: "Fear not!" Fear is so suffocating, demoralizing, and anxiety producing. It feels like a quiet death hovering over you. True faith and fear cannot exist in the same space together. But it is a real and constant tension that we must manage. So, what does the Bible say about fear versus faith?

Faith is described in Hebrews 11:1 as "the assurance of things hoped for, the conviction of things not seen." It is an absolute belief that God is present and constantly working behind the scenes in every area of our lives, even when there is no tangible evidence to support that fact. On the other hand, fear, simply stated, is unbelief. When we allow unbelief to gain the upper hand in our thoughts, fear takes hold of our emotions. Our deliverance from fear, worry, and anxiety is based on our faith, which is the very opposite of unbelief. We need to understand that faith is not something that we can produce in and of ourselves. Faith is a 100 percent free gift from God, but it requires our 100 percent surrender to receive it. In Galatians 5:22-23, faithfulness is described as a fruit (or characteristic) that is produced in our lives by the Holy Spirit. The Christian's faith is a confident assurance in a trustworthy God who loves us, knows our thoughts, and cares about our deepest needs. Our faith continues to grow as we study the Bible and learn the attributes of God's amazing character.

Fear has been defined as "false evidence appearing real," but there are also true scenarios that drive our fears; financial hardships, bad medical reports, broken-heartedness, addictions, loss, etc. I don't think that the way to fight fear is to ignore it, but rather to shine the light of our faith ON it. As we study the "fear not" passages of the Bible, we can navigate our fears and stand on our faith. The more we learn about God and see Him working in our lives, the stronger our faith grows. Fighting our fears with our faith will be the great antidote to fear ruling our lives. The fear feels so real. Our faith is real. The tension is real. Choose faith!

God promises us that we can experience peace in every situation. Philippians 4:7 says that His peace "surpasses all understanding" and "will guard your hearts and your minds in Christ Jesus." Choose your peace of mind. Die to your fear. Live by your faith.

Ponder:

How is the tension between your fears and your faith? What are some things you could do to die to your fears so that your faith can lead you with truth and peace?

Scriptures:

Isaiah 41:10

Fear not, for I am with you; be not dismayed, for I am your God; I will strengthen you, I will help you, I will uphold you with My righteous right hand.

Psalm 34:4

I sought the Lord, and He answered me and delivered me from all my fears.

Prayer:

Lord, help me increase my faith to navigate my fears. Help me to trust You when the outcome is not clear. I want to trust You as You strengthen me and hold me with Your righteous right hand. I want to "die" to myself in order to really live for You.

Day 5

Developing Our Faith

So, how can we increase faith to help conquer our fears? Romans 10:17 says, "Faith comes by hearing, and hearing by the Word of God." First John 4:18 says, "Perfect love casts out fear; that where there is love, there is no room for fear; and that the enemy of our Father and our souls has been defeated." As we learn more about God and read His Word, our eyes are opened to how He is working in our lives and strengthening our faith. God wants a relationship with us. He desires us to know Him and completely rely on His direction in our lives. By hearing, reading, and meditating in the Scriptures, we begin to experience a strong, confident faith that rejects worry and fear. This is our secret place. Spending intimate time in prayer and quiet study develops a relationship with our heavenly Father that sees us through even our darkest nights.

The Bible is also clear that our faith is matured and strengthened through trials. Like it or not, adversity is God's most effective tool to develop a strong faith. But we do not go through trials or fearful situations alone. He promises, "I am with you. I will never fail you. I will never abandon you" (Hebrews 13:5 NLT). As we learn to obey God's Word and allow it to saturate our thoughts, we find each trial becomes a stepping stone to increasing our faith. His faithfulness that sustained you in the past will strengthen, carry, and uphold you in the future.

The scripture is rich with promises that we can claim for ourselves to help us take hold of our fears as we develop our faith. Here are a few to keep in mind:

- **Financial trouble?** Philippians 4:19, "And my God will supply all your needs according to His riches in glory in Christ Jesus."

- **Rejection?** Romans 8:31, "If God is for us who can be against us!"

- **Personal fear?** Psalm 56:3, "When I am afraid, I will trust in You."

- **Fear about the future?** Psalm 32:8 "I will instruct you and teach you in the way you should go; I will counsel you with My eye upon you."

The list goes on and on. Scripture is full of His promises. Begin to memorize His promises. This is your solid ground. Even though we will continue to face various trials, God assures us that we can know a calm peace through every situation: "Do not be anxious about anything, but in every situation, by prayer and petition, with thanksgiving, present your requests to God. And the peace of God, which transcends all understanding, will guard your hearts and your minds in Christ Jesus" (Philippians 4:6-7). Die to your fears. Develop your faith.

Ponder:

How can I develop my faith through a closer relationship with the Lord? Do I recognize lies and truth as the scripture defines? How can I trust Him more in this area?

Scriptures:

1 Peter 5:7

Cast all your anxiety on Him, because He cares for you.

James 1:2-4

Consider it pure joy, my brothers and sisters, whenever you face trials of many kinds, because you know that the testing of your faith produces perseverance. Let perseverance finish its work so that you may be mature and complete, not lacking anything.

Prayer:

Lord, I want to know You more intimately so that I can trust You more. I want Your truths to be *my* truth. Shine Your light on the limiting beliefs and fears that can overwhelm me. I believe...help my unbelief. I want to "die" to myself in order to really live for You.

Day 6

Lies We Believe

*J*ust because you believe something doesn't make it true. Lies can be perceived as truth if you believe them to be so. Have you ever felt in your gut that you were being lied to but couldn't quite pinpoint it? This world has so many messages coming at us from every direction. Most are subtle lies from the prince of the world and the father of lies, Satan (John 8:44). Many start as simple misinformation early in our lives and then end up as ugly strongholds in later years.

The real tragedy of believing common lies is that the people of God do not follow and live in their God-given identity and destiny. We all fall into this trap in one way or another; no one is exempt. We all have been lied to by the media, by our bank account, by our past experiences, by our feelings, and even by loved ones around us. Our tendency is to allow our reason, emotions, or circumstances to dictate our truth as final authority. How do we identify these lies so that we can live in the truth? The Bible is the Lord's inspired Word, His holy instructions on how to combat the lies and live the sound life of truth, love, and peace. Second Timothy 3:16 says, "All Scripture is God-breathed and is useful for teaching, rebuking, correcting, and training in righteousness" Psalm 119:105 says, "Your word is a lamp for my feet, a light on my path." We invite the Holy Spirit, by a volitional act of faith, to cleanse and renew our minds so that we can stand on the truth and authority of God's word. As a child of God, we simply dare to believe that we are who HE says we are! As a Christian, we are not the same anymore. The old has gone and a new life has begun. When we become followers and believers in Jesus, we lose our identity in this world and embrace our new identity in Christ.

Memorize His power-filled truths to combat pervasive lies into your minds. When the truth is on the forefront of your mind, you will be more cognizant of the lies, and able to call them out and dismiss them. Imagine going onto a battlefield with no sword, no shield or helmet … that would be foolish. In the same way, we need to wear the FULL ARMOR OF GOD to conquer temptation and protect ourselves from the lies of the world. We must die to the lies we believe so that we can walk in HIS truths.

Ponder:

Identify areas where you are living below your Christian privilege as a child of God. Are you believing lies to be true? Die to the lies. Research the Bible for truths to shed a light on dark areas of your life.

Scriptures:

James 4:7

Submit yourselves, then, to God. Resist the devil, and he will flee from you.

Ephesians 6:10-12

Finally, be strong in the Lord and in His mighty power. Put on the full armor of God, so that you can take your stand against the devil's schemes. For our struggle is not against flesh and blood, but against the rulers, against the authorities, against the powers of this dark world and against the spiritual forces of evil in the heavenly realms.

Prayer:

Oh Lord, shed Your light on the subtle lies that I have believed to be true. Break these strongholds and reveal Your truths so that I may walk in them. I want to "die" to myself and to the lies in order to really live for You.

Day 7

Standing on the Truth

*G*od's Word is our solid ground for truth. It is the same yesterday, today, and forever. The truest thing about me is what God says, not what I think or feel and also not what others say, think, or project onto me. I have a new identity in Christ. I am who He says I am.

God's Word is true regardless of our past experiences, our own reason, emotions, performances, experiences, or circumstances. Joy is our birthright. Hope is our birthright. Love is our birthright. The scriptures are loaded with truth about our rightful Christian identity. Memorize them!

Here are a few of the common lies we believe and some truths in scripture to combat them:

- **I am not good enough** - You are a royal son/daughter of the King: 1 Peter 2:9, I am perfect in Christ: Heb. 10:14, Col. 2:10, Eph. 2:10

- **I am unloved** - You are very loved: John 15:9, Rom. 8:38-39, Eph. 2:4, 5:1-2

- **This is impossible. There seems to be no way** - Jesus IS the WAY and makes a way: John 14:6, Ps. 37:23, Jer. 29:11, Eph. 2:10

- **I am a fearful, anxious person** - I am free from fear: Ps. 34:4, 2 Tim. 1:7, 1 Peter 5:7, 1 John 4:18

- **I am not strong** - I have God's power and am indwelt by the Holy Spirit: Acts 1:8, Rom. 8:9-11, Eph. 1:18-19, Ps. 28:7

- **I do not have enough money for my needs** - God is Jehovah— that means provider. He will meet all of your needs for His glory! Philippians 4:19, Ps. 23:1

- **I can't make it? I don't know which way to go** - Pray to God,

He will show the right path. Seek His word; it will light your way. *Ps.119:105, Ps. 32:8,* Jer. 33:3

- **I am alone** -The LORD himself goes before you and will be with you; He will never leave you nor forsake you. Do not be afraid; do not be discouraged: Deut. 31:6, Ps. 73:23, Is. 41:10

You are called and equipped to do the good works that God has ordained you to do. Don't allow the enemy to use limiting beliefs or lies to rob, steal, and destroy your joy in your destiny. Die to the lies. Live in the truth. Choose and memorize His truth.

Ponder:

How much time do you spend memorizing power-filled truths to help navigate discouragement or lies in your life? Do you know your identity in Christ? Are you living on the solid ground of His truth?

Scriptures:

1 Peter 2:9

But you are a chosen people, a royal priesthood, a holy nation, God's special possession, that you may declare the praises of Him who called you out of darkness into His wonderful light.

Romans 8:38-39

For I am convinced that neither death nor life, neither angels nor demons, neither the present nor the future, nor any powers, neither height nor depth, nor anything else in all creation, will be able to separate us from the love of God that is in Christ Jesus our Lord.

Prayer:

Lord, I confess believing lies and not walking in the power of Your truths. Help me learn and hide Your truths in my heart so that I can live a life glorifying to You. I choose to believe you and not the lies from my enemy. I want to "die" to myself and walk in Your truth in order to really live for You.

Day 8
Opening Our Eyes

We all have choices to make daily. Yes or no? Now or later? This or that? Exercise or not? Eat healthy or not? Whine or not? Obey or not? Can we blame others for the choices that we make? Blaming never worked in the Garden of Eden and it doesn't work in life either. We also choose our thoughts and our focus. Experience has taught me that my heart was not made for the weight of anxiety, depression, and fear. I know that I thrive with life, hope, and joy. Do we have any say so in this process? Or are we simply a victim of our lives? Can we choose to be victors instead of victims? One of the biggest game changers for my life has been my intentional decision to "focus on that which is praiseworthy."

When I married my husband, I focused on all that I loved about him and was delighted to say "YES" till death do us part. Then life happened. I found myself deeply frustrated with our relationship. How could this be? What changed? I wasn't alert to the subtle and sneaky ways of the enemy. I found myself easily diverted and ended up focusing on the "lack" in my man. So why? My marriage was uplifting for so long and then it felt heavy and draining. Who could I blame? Of course, I wanted to blame him. My pastor reminded me that our lives will always move in the direction of our strongest thoughts and that we find what we are looking for. I was focusing on all the ways my husband wasn't living up to who I thought he should be and all that he wasn't doing! Even if it was true, it was killing our marriage. I began desperately looking for the things that I DID love about my husband, the reasons that I said "YES," the reasons I chose him. I made a choice, to change what I was looking *at*. I was on a pursuit for "all that was praiseworthy" about him. It was a game-changer for our marriage. My husband hadn't changed, but I had changed my focus which ultimately changed the environment in our home. As I spoke life-giving words from my new focus, life returned to my marriage.

The strategic choice of obedience to "focus on the praiseworthy" applies to many other areas of life as well. As I changed my focus at my job, things suddenly got better. As I changed my focus about my children, they became more lovable. I noticed a distinct trend. My obedience was rewarded. This became a solid reality in my life. Since I don't thrive in heaviness, ugliness, lying, deceit, or destruction, I truly limit negative things in my life. I find that trash "*in*" leads to trash "*out*." Die to the negative truths in your life and pursue a life of focusing on that which is praiseworthy.

Ponder:

How can you focus more on the blessings in your life, your people, and your circumstances? Consider asking the Lord to help blind you to the negative, draining places in your life.

Scriptures:

1 Peter 5:8

Be alert and of sober mind. Your enemy the devil prowls around like a roaring lion looking for someone to devour.

Philippians 4:8

Finally, brothers and sisters, whatever is true, whatever is noble, whatever is right, whatever is pure, whatever is lovely, whatever is admirable—if anything is excellent or praiseworthy—think about such things.

Prayer:

Lord, open my eyes to that which is good, pure, and praiseworthy. Help me focus on Your daily blessings and not on those life-draining things that I cannot control. Help me choose to see Your fingerprint of blessing everywhere in my days. I want to "die" to myself in order to really live for You.

Day 9
The Death of My Vision

*H*ave you ever had a dream/vision that died? In the biblical story of Joseph, we see that Joseph had a dream of his family bowing down to him (Gen. 37:5-9). But God had greater purposes than Joseph could have hoped or imagined. I had a dream too. Maybe you did as well. Do our dreams line up with His greater purposes?

As his story goes, starting in Genesis 37, Joseph found himself in a pit, sold as a slave, falsely accused and more. This was not in Joseph's original vision/dream. These events looked like the "death of the vision." Are there things in your life that look like the "death of your vision," too? But GOD! He was with Joseph. He is with you. He never leaves us, fails us or forsakes us. He never wastes a thing.

The Lord's plan is a perfect one, even when it doesn't match up with our plans. The Lord knows all—past, present and future—and He only wants the absolute best for His children. When you die to your SELF and let Him have control, life will become an even more beautiful journey. When we are experiencing the "death of a vision," we have to consider that the sweet Lord is beckoning us to His greater vision and purposes.

Just as the vinedresser trims the dead things off of the vine so that it can bear more and greater fruit, God may have to cut away some of our self-centered dreams to make room for His bigger and better purposes for our lives. This could be called a purposeful pruning or a divine downsizing. I have experienced this personally. During an extremely challenging and heart-breaking season of my life, God birthed a new, fresh vision and compassion in my heart. He stripped away my old, limited visions for a grander plan. I had to die so that I could live.

The Lord loves us enough to help us with our distorted priorities or superficial motives. This purifying process often strips away our ego and pride to leave a beautiful gift of a totally yielded heart for His greater call. Just like Joseph, we may experience more than one death of a vision. God often takes away something good from our lives to create room for something better. What the enemy means for evil the Lord can turn for good. Sometimes we have to give up what we want NOW for what we want even MORE. I ultimately want to live in the sweet center of God's will for my life.

If the death of our self-centered limited vision can bring us into more fullness of His purposes for our lives, then may we die so that we can live.

Ponder:

How can you yield your dreams and hope for His greater glory? Are you willing to die to your plan if it can yield His greater purposes? Do you trust Him?

Scriptures:

Proverbs 19:21

Many are the plans in a person's heart, but it is the Lord's purpose that prevails.

Ephesians 3:20

Now to Him who is able to do immeasurably more than all we ask or imagine, according to His power that is at work within us.

Prayer:

Lord, I need to know that You are close. Whenever my plans seem to fall apart, help me trust that You can and will work all things together for a greater good. I love You and want Your greater purposes for my life. I want to "die" to myself in order to really live for You.

Living "FROM" Him versus "FOR" Him

*O*ur beliefs are the water we swim in. It is easy to sometimes feel like the weight of the world is on our shoulders. We try our hardest to live the best life possible. Then, we try even harder. Years ago, I was in a very desperate place in my life. So many of life's disappointments were piling higher and higher. It felt like I was carrying the weight of a piano on my shoulders. I was overwhelmed and exhausted. I was ready and more than willing to hear God's whispers for newness and freedom. But I just tried harder. I was attempting to live "right" by living righteous. Doing all the right things but often getting the wrong results. How could this be? I was running so hard, juggling so much, and spinning so many plates. Don't I get an "A" for effort?

How many of us grew up on the "performance treadmill?" Trying to be "good for God?" This is truly an exercise in exhaustion. We often feel empty and never quite enough. We are always enough when He lives *through* us for His greater purposes. We are rarely enough when we live in our own strength. His Holy Spirit is the gift in us. Christ in us is our hope for glory!

God's work WITHIN you prepares you for Him to work THROUGH you. This transformation is 100 percent the work of God and 100 percent your yielding to it. The true mystery is living FROM Him instead of the exhaustion of living FOR Him … You know, that exhausting treadmill of trying harder?

Amidst my hardest and darkest season of absolute exasperation and fatigue, I was led to a beautiful surrender and a new freedom in Christ. I decided to let go of living *from* my capabilities, behaviors, environment, or even my limiting beliefs. The dear Lord wants our whole heart, our whole mind, and our whole soul so much that He is willing to rip everything away until there is nothing left but a sweet emptiness that demands that we lay at rest in His arms … finally FREE.

This is our dying to live. This is where our weakness yields way to His strength within. This is where we actually begin to live FROM Him *within* instead of living FOR Him *without*. You want this freedom. Don't wait until you have the weight of the world on your shoulders to live from this freedom. Quit simply trying harder. Let Him carry the load. Die to live.

Ponder:

What would life be like if we cast all our burdens on Him and let His Holy Spirit carry us through? Do you have the weight of the world on your shoulders? Give Him your burdens. Live FROM His strength and His call, not on the performance treadmill.

Scriptures:

John 14:20

On that day you will realize that I am in my Father, and you are in Me, and I am in you.

Galatians 2:20

I have been crucified with Christ and I no longer live, but Christ lives in me. The life I now live in the body, I live by faith in the Son of God, who loved me and gave Himself for me.

Prayer:

Oh Lord, I am exhausted by trying to spin all of the plates of performance. Save me from myself. I die to myself living FOR You and ask that You fill me "to overflowing" so that I can live FROM Your strength and purposes. I want to "die" to myself in order to really live for You.

CHAPTER 5

Voices and Choices

*I*f we are the product of the voices and influences we choose to listen to, who are you on your way to becoming?

If you're anything like me, you live with a constant barrage of voices from yourself, the Lord, the enemy, your boss, your husband, your kids, your girlfriends, your parents, and the random woman at the grocery store. This plethora of voices can often feel like a battlefield in your mind. You will have to make a choice … to listen to anyone and everyone that screams your name or take a stand for truth.

Day 1
Identifying the Battlefield

*E*very single day there is a battle in and around your mind between good and evil. Honestly, half of winning the battle is just being aware that there is one. Some days it is totally obvious, but other days it is subtle or not even noticeable. God's Word makes it very clear that there is evil in the world today, and we are in a battle for our souls. This unseen battle is not of flesh and blood but of the spirit (Ephesians 6:10-12). Even though we cannot see this battle, none-the-less, it is real.

There are many "fronts" to our battlefield. Most of our battles are in our mind but affect our actions. They are the *voices* that lead us to daily *choices*. Many of us engage in emotional battles especially dealing with love, pain, or disappointment. Then there are the intellectual battles. Also consider the physical battles of what to eat, how to eat, and how to stay healthy in such an unhealthy world. There are also the financial battles we face questioning provision. Clearly the most significant is the spiritual battlefield. Ultimately this is an eternal life or death battle. Christians find their final and ultimate security in Christ; however, there is a real, day-to-day battle of flesh versus spirit which affects our peace of mind. All these "voices" can confuse our daily choices.

Since we have an enemy, all of God's people fight this same fight. You are not alone.

Paul urges us to "put on the full armor of God so that you can take your stand against the devil's schemes." Paul goes on to encourage us to not fear evil because Jesus has already overcome Satan and the world. We are overcomers. We can stand strong with the full armor of God so that we are able to defeat Satan's attempts to destroy us. God has equipped us with everything we need to fight the good fight!

For me, half the battle was just becoming AWARE of the battle. This is not a "one and done" fight. It is an ongoing daily fight. We can't just "get it and set it." With the dawn of each new day, we must set our minds on the eternal and not the temporal. Choose this day whom you will serve! Arm yourself with life-giving truths. Take all other thoughts captive!

Ponder:

How are you aware of this daily battlefield of voices and choices? In what ways can you start your days prepared for the battle?

Scriptures:

Ephesians 6:10-13

Finally, be strong in the Lord and in His mighty power. Put on the full armor of God, so that you can take your stand against the devil's schemes. For our struggle is not against flesh and blood, but against the rulers, against the authorities, against the powers of this dark world and against the spiritual forces of evil in the heavenly realms. Therefore, put on the full armor of God, so that when the day of evil comes, you may be able to stand your ground, and after you have done everything, to stand.

Colossians 3:1-2

Since, then, you have been raised with Christ, set your hearts on things above, where Christ is, seated at the right hand of God. Set your minds on things above, not on earthly things.

Prayer:

Lord, thank you for giving us weapons of warfare, for showing us the true battle is not of this earthly world. Show us the true source of our struggles and help us to find victory in Your Word and Your ways. I choose Your voice over all the other voices.

Day 2

The Voices We Hear

*T*here are four voices that are raging in our heads on a daily basis. Another way to put this internal battle could be "The Battle of the Wills." No wonder there can be confusion in our lives. No wonder people can be at odds with one another. No wonder that there can never truly be "peace on earth."

These four wills/voices are:

1. **The will/voice of God the Father.** God designed each of us ON purpose, WITH purpose, and FOR a purpose. He is the Knitter and the Knower of each day of our lives. We are fearfully and wonderfully made. He designed that we walk in an intimate relationship with Him. He is constantly knocking at the door of our heart as He longs to speak to us.

2. **The will/voice of the enemy.** We do have an enemy of our souls—a thief, who comes to rob, kill, and destroy our lives, our joy, our families, and His will. He seeks death over life and wants to destroy all that is good and right. He is sneaky. He is real.

3. **The will/voice of ourselves.** Then we have to deal with our own self-will, our own selfish nature, and our own pride that wants our own way. We all have the common ground of the "human condition." We all have blind spots. We all are self-centered to some degree.

4. **The will/voice of the other.** This could be our parents, teacher, boss, neighbor, friend, or pastor. There are often many voices in our lives telling us what to do. Or even just suggesting what to do. Most of these voices mean well, but they are still other voices that we hear.

After watching this battle in my life for over half a century, I have come to realize just how real it is. Believe me, I have contemplated the choices. Stop and think about the four voices listed above. Upon considering these daily choices, it seems easy to determine the best choice would be His will, His way. Years ago, I decided to start a new daily habit. My first thought in the morning is to say (in the same spirit of Jesus), "Not my will, but Thine, be done." Then I welcome the Lord's divine interruptions into my day. We know that His plans are greater than anything we could hope or imagine. Choose to yield to the voice of the One. Choose God's will in God's way.

Pay attention! Slow down and listen to the voice of the Father. Be aware of the other voices and the choices as the voice you believe will determine the future you experience.

Ponder:

Do you feel a tug-of-war inside you over certain issues? Is your life often confusing? Consider the daily prayer for His will, His way versus your will, your way.

Scriptures:

John 10:10

The thief comes only to steal and kill and destroy; I have come that they may have life and have it to the full.

Ephesians 3:20

Now to Him who is able to do immeasurably more than all we ask or imagine, according to His power that is at work within us ...

Prayer:

Oh Lord, Help us to live for Your voice only. Help me to hear Your voice. Deafen me to the voice of the enemy of my soul. I hunger to live out Your will, Your way every day. I choose Your voice over all the other voices.

Day 3

Vantage Points

*Y*ears ago, there was a TV movie called "Vantage Point." It was a fictional movie about the attempted assassination of an American president. The movie was replayed to the viewer from different "vantage points," and the story was different each time. Parlaying the vantage point idea into our own personal lives, have you ever remembered a personal story and have another person say, "That is not how it was?" My children often remember some of their life stories very differently than I, their mother. So, who is right? Is the story how I remember it to be or how they thought it was? Perspective is truth to the owner. What a giant idea to ponder.

There is a statement, "Seek first to understand and then to be understood." The wisdom gained from this statement enhances our understanding of the vantage point idea. Seeing things from the position of another person will enhance greater understanding and empathy. Not necessarily agreement. But certainly, more understanding!

Since God is the Creator and the Knower, I want His vantage point. If only we could see our days from the viewpoint of our Loving Father God … His eternal perspective and plan. It is easy to be limited in our vantage point as we are limited creatures. We do not understand many things.

Proverbs 3:5-6 tells us to lean not on our own understanding but to trust Him in all things. Oftentimes, this scripture helps me reckon with the unreasonable circumstances in life. I draw myself to consider an eternal perspective and not one from my limited point-of-view. In the Bible, Jesus actually admonished the disciples when they were "seeing things from a human point of view and not from God's eternal point of view." We must set our perspective and our minds on things above, not on earthly things. This requires us to walk by faith and not by sight. The more solid our faith and trust, the more solid our days.

Life is enormously easier for me whenever I am choosing a quiet resolve and a confident trust in the viewpoint of the Trustworthy One. He alone is Sovereign. Now I challenge myself to always consider the eternal perspective of the moment. I have become accustomed to the thought of trusting God's eternal vantage point. This trust affords me greater peace-of-mind.

Ponder:

How can you take time to consider another person's truth, perspective, or point of view to help build your relationship with them? What are some ways for you to surrender your understanding of things and ask God for His eternal perspective?

Scriptures:

Proverbs 3:5-6

Trust in the Lord with all your heart and lean not on your own understanding; in all your ways submit to Him, and He will make your paths straight.

Galatians 1:10
Am I now trying to win the approval of human beings, or of God? Or am I trying to please people? If I were still trying to please people, I would not be a servant of Christ.

Prayer:

Lord, I want your eternal vantage point, especially when I do not understand. Teach me Your ways. Help me to trust You and Your sovereign plans. I choose Your voice over all the other voices.

Day 4

Who Can I Blame?

We simply cannot blame others for our choices. We are responsible for our own actions and behaviors, not for the behaviors of others. Blame and shame started in the Garden of Eden and were not a part of God's original design of peace and harmony. We hear the old phrase, "The devil made me do it." The truth is that our enemy is a deceiver in every way! Even though the devil tempted Eve and Adam with the words, "Did God really say …?", it was their choice, in response to the enemy's voice, that changed their entire world. They entered a world of shame and blame. We live in that world today.

God knows our human condition. He knows that we are sinners. Through Christ, He has provided a saving grace so that we can live our life more abundantly. Because we all have the freedom of choice, we simply must take responsibility for our own actions. The Holy Spirit within gives us the strength to make wise choices as we pray for the wisdom to do so.

Oftentimes, it is difficult for us to take personal responsibility for our poor choices. We might be embarrassed. We might feel pressure or desperation. We might feel shame. We have a myriad of excuses all leading to blame. We can only change and improve our lives to the degree that we are willing to accept responsibility for our actions. Everyone's life is messy. But the buck stops with us. I cannot blame away the results of my life.

One of the marks of Christian maturity is taking personal responsibility. This does not include finger-pointing or blaming others. I used to teach our kids, "All choices have consequences so choose very carefully." The choice to blame is not a healthy choice as it separates and breaks down relationships.

Although we have no power to control what others do or say, we do have the Holy Spirit to help us govern how we respond. We are not in charge of the actions and behavior of others. We are not in charge of the news. We are not in charge of the weather. We are not in charge of so much, but we are in charge of our responses. Oftentimes, we try to blame our response on the behaviors of others. WE justify our actions with blame statements like, "But he made me so mad!" In reality, we choose to become angry whether justifiably so or not.

Each of us is accountable to Him for both our attitude and our responses. We may think that the blame game makes us look better but the Lord is not fooled. If we are clinging to blame, we are simply hanging onto an emotional weakness that separates us from God. The responses He desires from us are forgiveness when we are hurt and repentance when we have sinned against another person. Let's endeavor to stop the blame game. It leads nowhere.

Ponder:

How could you identify blame, shame, and poor choices in your own life? How can you take more personal responsibility for each of your daily choices? Stop blaming others for your responses and ask God to strengthen you with patience and wisdom.

Scriptures:

Genesis 3:12-13

The man said, "The woman You put here with me—she gave me some fruit from the tree, and I ate it." Then the Lord God said to the woman, "What is this you have done?" The woman said, "The serpent deceived me, and I ate."

Luke 14:27

And whoever does not carry their cross and follow Me cannot be my Disciple.

Prayer:

Oh Lord! I don't want to be a whiner or a blamer. Help me identify and eliminate these poor choices. I want to take personal responsibility for my behavior and respond with Your love. I choose Your voice over all the other voices.

Day 5

The Voice Above All Voices

We live in a noisy world full of voices and choices. But Jesus, our Shepherd, calls us by name and leads us in the paths that we should follow. He stands at the door of our hearts and knocks, waiting for us to invite Him into relationship with Him. We must quiet the noises, lean in, and choose to hear THE Voice above all other voices.

I wish that this was an easy proposition. Our hearts are still too full of the clamor of the world and its false values. Recognizing the true voice of the Shepherd is not so easy if you are not in relationship with Him. We recognize the voice of our spouse on the phone since we are in a daily relationship with them. It is a rich blessing to hear the voice of the One who knows us deeply and loves us unconditionally.

The Lord is always speaking. He longs to speak to us personally. He speaks to us in a heart language that we can hear and understand. Invite Him to speak to you and then sit quietly, be still, and listen. Find a quiet place and open your ears for this important conversation. Sometimes it is a whisper. Invite the Holy Spirit to clear out your ears and turn up the volume.

One key to hearing God's voice is to go to a quiet place and still our own thoughts and emotions. Psalm 46:10 encourages us to be still, let go, cease striving, and know that He is God. In Psalm 37:7, we are called to "be still before the Lord and wait patiently for Him." There is a deep inner knowing in our spirits that we can each experience when we quiet our flesh and our minds. Relax in His healing, holy presence. Allow Him to transform you through this quiet time of listening.

Another key to hearing God's voice is through prayer and fixing the eyes of our heart upon Jesus and His ways. Invite God to reveal Himself to you and speak to your heart. Open this conversation. Open the eyes of your heart, look internally, and purpose to seek His ways and next steps.

Spending time in God's Word will amplify our confidence to hear His voice. His Word is sharper than a two-edged sword and is full of His righteous teachings. Invite His Holy Spirit into this process to help His voice come alive through His Word. Then top it off with journaling or the writing out of our prayers and God's answers. A prayer journal can bring additional freedom in hearing His voice.

Set your antenna to hear His voice above all the other noise in your world. Listen in to the voice of the ONE who knows you best and loves you most.

Ponder:

What are some ways that you can quiet the noise in your life in order to hear THE voice of the Lord's leading? He wants to talk to you. Open the eyes of your heart to hear the voice of the ONE.

Scriptures:

Luke 11:28

He replied, "Blessed rather are those who hear the word of God and obey it."

John 10:27-28

My sheep listen to My voice; I know them, and they follow Me. I give them eternal life, and they shall never perish; no one will snatch them out of My hand.

Prayer:

Oh Lord, I want to hear Your voice above all of the drowning noise in my world. Help me quiet my activities and my heart to tune into Your loving whispers and guidance. I choose Your voice over all the other voices.

CHAPTER 6

Voices of the Enemy

*A*nyone else sick and tired of the exhausting, crippling lies berating your heart? The lies that say you are unworthy, unseen, and unloved? The lies that say you don't measure up? The lies that say you are alone and forsaken?

One of the lies I've battled throughout my life is believing I'm less than God says I am. Believing that I'm an unqualified mother, an unworthy wife, and an unwanted friend. Those things are SUCH a lie! But it's crazy, sometimes I'm still tempted to believe them. That's why we have to be diligent in checking our beliefs against the truth, not just accepting whatever we feel. Who are we gonna believe? Let's shine a light on common lies of our enemy. Let's not participate in the enemy's schemes.

Day 1

The Voice of Fear

*T*he enemy of our souls wants us to live a life crippled by fear. Fear is a distressing emotion that is aroused by impending danger, evil, pain, etc., whether the threat is real or imagined. Of course, the enemy of your heart wants you to be timid and afraid! Time and again, we live life holding the nerve-racking hand of fear versus holding the peace-filled hand of the Father. Do we have a choice in this matter? Who are we to blame for the grip of fear in our lives?

Second Timothy 1:7 is a popular verse to keep in mind when dealing with fear. This verse brings us the understanding that God didn't give us the spirit of fear, but of power, love, and self-discipline (or sound mind in some translations). Our fears can cause us to trust in things, people, places, idols, etc., instead of trusting in the One who created and breathed them into life. Fear causes your mind and judgment to be clouded, leading you to make decisions that you wouldn't have made if you had a clear head about the situation. So, in the face of fear, God reminds us that we were created to love, to be strong, and to be clear-headed. We must choose the Voice of Truth and to seek Him and this solid ground. As we choose a sound mind over fear, we will have to speak supporting truths in the place of the lies. Scripture is filled with truth and promises to navigate the voice of fear.

Your mind is somewhat like a seesaw that teeters and totters. As your trust in God goes up, your fear and worry go down. Time spent with the Lord not only increases your trust; it also helps you discern truth from fear.

F.E.A.R. has been referred to as "False Evidence Appearing Real." When gripped with fear, my internal control-freak rises. When I realize that I cannot control the thing I fear, then I fear even more, and the circle goes around and around. Fear can push the most composed people into states of utter discomfort and uncertainty, but God reminds people through His Word that because of Jesus, there is nothing to fear.

I want to act out of a quiet, confident peace rather than the voice of fear shadowing my days. Let us walk in the truth that the Lord is with us wherever we go and will strengthen us as we yield to Him. He offers a peace that surpasses all understanding, but it is up to us to choose this peace by ultimately trusting Him. Face down your fears in the light of God's truths. Let's walk in His peace, leading to our sound mind.

Ponder:

How am I letting the voice of fear rob the wise decision making in my days? Where is fear crippling my life? What truths can help me navigate to solid ground?

Scripture:

Joshua 1:9

Have I not commanded you? Be strong and courageous. Do not be afraid; do not be discouraged, for the Lord your God will be with you wherever you go.

Psalm 34:4

I sought the Lord, and He answered me; He delivered me from all my fears.

Prayer:

Oh Lord, help me live a life of power, love, and a sound mind, focusing on Your power in my life and not the voice of fear. I want to be strong and courageous. Deliver me from my fears. Help me recognize fear as a voice of the liar.

Day 2

The Voice of Anxiety

*T*he voice of anxiety can be a sister to the voice of fear, causing the same distress, uneasiness, and restlessness. It can hit us from all directions, whether it be school, work, family, or other unsettling circumstances. Anxiety is another crippling voice that can leave us feeling overwhelmed, panicked, nervous, and uncertain. This is no way to live. Amidst our anxiety, our control freak nature feels out-of-control. Did we ever really have control anyway? So often control is truly an illusion. We lose our peace as well as our peace-of-mind. What are we doing?

As with fear, anxiety starts us on an exhausting cycle. When we feel anxious about something, we generally try to do all that is in our power to control the situation. When we can't control it, we become even more anxious. So how do we stop this downward spiral of anxious turmoil?

We must release our anxious heart to the One who is in control of all things. He is Sovereign, and we are not. God holds all of our lives in His hands and is the only One who can truly calm our anxious hearts and minds. When we frantically struggle to put the pieces of our lives together on our own, we will fail.

The word tells us to be anxious for nothing … no thing! I have learned when my heart starts to palpitate with the onslaught of anxiety to STOP, DROP, and WORSHIP. This breaks the reign of anxiety in my heart and transfers that spotlight back to my Lord who is worthy. He inhabits the praises of His people, and my anxious heart simply needs a load of His "inhabiting." I need to reframe my heart to a heart choosing a quiet resolve and a confident trust in the Trustworthy One. He does a better job everyday anyway! I actively remind myself to rest in "His will, His way" vs "my will, my way" as He can make all things work together for my good.

Remember, all you can do is all you can do. You must trust God to do that which you cannot do. In your weakness, He is your strength. Can you let go of your grip of control, or the lack thereof, to trust His peace and provision?

Ponder:

How is the weight of your anxiety exhausting you? Do you have enough time and energy to spend on things beyond your control? How can you choose more peace of mind?

Scriptures:

Philippians 4:6-7

Do not be anxious about anything, but in every situation, by prayer and petition, with thanksgiving, present your requests to God. And the peace of God, which transcends all understanding, will guard your hearts and your minds in Christ Jesus.

Isaiah 41:10

So do not fear, for I am with you; do not be dismayed, for I am your God. I will strengthen you and help you; I will uphold you with My righteous right hand.

Prayer:

Oh Lord, help me be anxious for NOTHING and trust You with EVERYTHING today. I bring my overwhelming exhaustion to Your feet and resolve to trust in You. You are trustworthy and I need rest. Quiet the voice of my anxious heart with Your unconditional love and truth. Help me recognize anxiety as a voice of the liar.

Day 3

The Voice of Comparison

Comparison is the thief of joy. Oftentimes, comparing ourselves to others also leads us into making poor choices. Each of us are unique. God created each of us fearfully and wonderfully and then signed us with our own unique thumbprint. We are not like other people. We were not designed to be them. Not to look like them or live like them. Not to carry their load. We have a unique call upon our lives to be totally and completely who He created us to be. Don't get distracted by unnecessary and unwanted comparisons. Stay on your own path.

Comparing ourselves to others is an ugly game that we all have played, and it leads to the death of our happiness. Envy can often be the result of this comparison game, and God does not like envy. There is no win in this game. No finish line. No final satisfaction. Keep your eyes to yourself, your giftings, and your call. Live for the audience of ONE. Listen to only His voice. Do not carry more than what you are called to do. Unload your backpack from the unwanted comparisons in your life.

The only true antidote to comparison is contentment, which begins with a thankful heart. The comparison trap compels us to turn inward, to focus on ourselves, what we lack, what caused our lack or discontentment. Thankfulness, on the other hand, compels us to turn our attention to others. It's like a salve over a fragile or damaged heart from too many comparisons. When we are thankful, we don't see what we lack. Instead, we see the generosity and faithfulness of a good Father and are compelled to meet the needs of others.

The internet and social media can wreak havoc and amp up comparison to either discourage you or encourage you all in the same breath. It's so easy to scroll and scroll and have disappointment and jealousy grow with every thumb swipe as we overanalyze and scrutinize the lives of others. Our peace of mind only comes with trusting the Knitter and the Knower for our perfectly imperfect individual design. He gifted each of us uniquely to bless and serve others. Do not be an "elbow" trying to be a "foot" in the body of Christ. We are all geniuses at something, but if a fish spent his lifetime trying to climb a tree, he would feel stupid. Stay in your lane. You are uniquely created to shine as you, and you alone.

Instead of checking your social media accounts, "Delight yourselves in the Lord," knowing "he will give you the desires of your heart" (Psalm 37:4).

Ponder:

How is comparison a "thief of your joy?" How can you see discontent settling in your heart by too much TV or social media? Thank God for your uniquely gifted self and honor Him with gladness.

Scriptures:

Galatians 1:10

Am I now trying to win the approval of human beings, or of God? Or am I trying to please people? If I were still trying to please people, I would not be a servant of Christ.

Galatians 6:4

Each one should test their own actions. Then they can take pride in themselves alone, without comparing themselves to someone else.

Prayer:

O Lord, blind me to comparing myself to others and help me to understand exactly who You created me to be. Lead me into my own unique purpose that You designed just for me. Help me recognize comparison as a voice of the liar.

Day 4

The Voice of Inadequacy

I wrote a different Bible plan called *The Lie of Not Enough*. It addresses my questions of sufficiency for God's call upon my life. I even wrote a book called *Are You Enough?* Crazy just how common is this lie of insufficiency. Now I am not talking about being capable of actually doing things beyond my ability like running 100 miles. I am addressing the common lie of not being able to handle that which God purposes us to do. He calls us to love Him and love others. But whenever God puts a burden on our hearts, He will open a door to accomplish His will.

Sometimes this lie of inadequacy is a sister to the voice of comparison. We peek over the fence into another's life and are hit with an onslaught of inadequate thoughts. We are not to be like others but like our BEST self. The Word says that we have all sufficiency to do every good work that He has called us to do. Don't exhaust yourself taking on more than you are called to. Be wise and highly selective in your "YESes."

As a wife and a mom, I often wrestle with an exhausting lie that I cannot love well. I have come to realize that in my flesh, that is true. When I die to my selfish nature and ask the Lord to live through me, I have more than enough love. I simply need to get myself out of His way of greater love. He must become more and more, and I must become less and less to live in the abundance of His purposes for my life. His capacity for love is limitless and my capacity of love is very limited. My adequacy comes from His indwelling Spirit living through me and yielding the fruits of His Spirit to others. My sufficiency depends on my dependence on Him to give me His strength to live His will, His way. His yoke is light. Yoke up with Him alone!

How do you respond when you sense the Lord is calling you to a task that seems overwhelming and beyond your abilities? Do you mentally list all the reasons you can't possibly do it? God already knows everything about you and the situation at hand. He's not asking your permission to proceed; rather, He is calling you to move forward into a greater faith and obedience. He didn't make an error in choosing you for His assigned tasks. He wants to show you His power through your submission.

God has equipped you for whatever He calls you to do. Because the Holy Spirit dwells within every believer, we have all we need to fulfill the Lord's mission and purposes. Instead of letting inadequacy hinder you from obeying, let it drive you to your knees so you can arise with His renewed insight and power.

Ponder:

How can I live a life intentionally dependent on His abundant love and power living through me? What are some ways that I can choose confidence in His mission and purposes for my life?

Scriptures:

2 Corinthians 9:8

And God is able to bless you abundantly, so that in all things at all times, having all that you need, you will abound in every good work.

2 Corinthians 3:4-6

Such confidence we have through Christ before God. Not that we are competent in ourselves to claim anything for ourselves, but our competence comes from God. He has made us competent as ministers of a new covenant—not of the letter but of the Spirit; for the letter kills, but the Spirit gives life.

Prayer:

Lord, help me to live in Your sufficiency in all things at all times so that I can abound in every good work that You have intended for me. Help me recognize inadequacy as a voice of the liar.

Day 5

The Voice of Confusion

*A*re you ever confused? What does it mean to live FROM Him versus living FOR Him? Well, let this performance treadmill queen explain some things that it does NOT mean. I spent most of my life believing that I had to be "good enough" to get into heaven ... totally a works mentality! Then with social media ramping up, I had to deal with the life-sucking, joy-robbing weight of comparison on top of it all. As a young adult, my thoughts that "I wanted my parents to be proud of me" went way overboard into a deep exhausting drive for more. Pridefully juggling all the "balls" became a way of life. Little did I know that it would become a sure road to loads of stress.

After having four kids in five years, the performance treadmill really began to speed up. Oh, and let's not talk about all the things the kids should be involved in and doing. You know, those things to give them experience, maturity, and friendships like sports, dance, piano, church activities, community service projects, etc. Even just marriage itself adds levels of work. Now ... to really put a cherry on top, we pulled all four of our kids out of school and started homeschooling them immediately after we moved states. Am I crazy or what? In hindsight it sounds almost laughable, like choosing to live in a nuthouse of stress and busyness.

Do you realize that a fish swimming in water never gets tired? You know why? Because a fish is designed to live and swim in water! Simple enough? So, if a fish never gets tired, and I was living exhausted spiritually and emotionally then where in the heck is my "fishness" and where in the heck is my water? I want to "not live tired." Who could I blame for my tiredness? Could I blame my husband? My children? When in doubt, always blame your mother! It would have been laughable if it wasn't so pitiful.

I realized that I couldn't blame anyone for MY choices and MY responses to life. Ugh. The ball sits square in my corner. No blame. So I embarked on a journey of deep intimacy with the Lord to rediscover my "fishness" or my gifts and talents. I purposed to leave my crazy busy world and to crawl up into His arms and have a long intimate chat. When I told Him that I was exhausted and DONE being exhausted, He said, "Are you sure you are done? My yoke is easy and My burden is light." What? How smart did I have to be? Sure, I am done Lord! I am drowning in all my own decisions. My blessings and my choices are completely exhausting me.

The sweet Lord invited me into what seemed like a "slow dance"… a place of safety, security, love and renewal … off the treadmill. He wanted to hold me and whisper in my ears. He wanted me and me alone. He wanted my undivided attention. He wanted to restore what the locusts had eaten in my life … to make beauty from ashes and give me new mercies each morning. He reminded me that if I didn't slow down, I left no room for Him to do the miracle. He invited me. He invites you. He reminded me that upon asking Him to be the Lord of my life that His Holy Spirit entered the picture as my personal helper. His Spirit. His Holiness. If I would stay in the intimate place of relationship with Him, He would do His work through me. He would sustain my days and carry the load. His power working within me enables me to "swim like a fish in water," not getting so tired. I gave Him my heavy yoke and humbly invited Him, in a new way, to be my all. He is always willing. Now I was ready. I wanted to live FROM the place of His overflowing strength and power through. I wanted to stop living FOR Him with all my good ideas. Free at last? Yes, if I choose to remain IN HIM. But there are days that I "take it back." Why in the world would I do such? Every morning now, I purposefully choose to die to myself and my ideas so that He can live through me with His purposes for that day. I invite His "Divine interruptions." I let Him carry my burdens for the day.

I invite you to learn with me … to breath in the Holy Spirit power that has been given to you. Live from this place of freedom and rest instead of carrying around your all-important life. Live in your Christian privilege … Christ in you, the hope of glory! It's time to breathe!

Ponder:

How often do you run on the performance treadmill just trying harder and harder to keep up? Have you ever blamed others for the choices that you make? Are you close enough with the Lord that you can hear His guiding voice?

Scriptures:

1 Corinthians 14:33

For God is not a God of disorder but of peace—as in all the congregations of the Lord's people

Psalm 119:114

You are my refuge and my shield; I have put my hope in your word.

Prayer:

Oh Lord, I want Your indwelling Holy Spirt to lead, guide and direct my days. I want to live at peace resting in Your "next steps" for my life. Thank You for never failing or forsaking me. I want to live as Your vessel of purpose and power. Help me recognize confusion as a voice of the liar.

Day 6

Other Voices of the Liar

We are created in the image of God. It's Our Father's desire that we remember and live by our true identity every day. However, the enemy of our souls is a liar and lives to deceive us! Be on guard! We must know the Truth! He only comes to steal, kill, and destroy our joy, our family, and our purpose.

As a believer, our identity in Christ is full of life. The lies of our flesh often bring a feeling of death. Life in Christ can offer peace, patience, joy, rest, fulfillment, love, purpose and satisfaction. A life lived in the flesh often yields irritability, anger, bitterness, criticism, depression, judgement, anxiety, and other ugly emotions. These are weighty lies!

A study of our identity in Christ as a believer is a study in His truth over the enemy's lies. We must walk in the Voice of Truth. It can be found in the Word. We must know the scriptures, memorize the truths, and hide them in our hearts. This equips us to live in this daily battlefield of the voices and the choices.

If you are at a place of questioning your identity, then the most important thing is to NOT let your circumstances define you. Speak these five identity truths and remember them when the challenges of this life overshadow your heart and mind:

1. **I Am Chosen by God (Ephesians 1:4)** - "I'm special in God's eyes. He chose me to be complete in Him even before this world was created. I am called as an individual."

2. **I Am Fearfully and Wonderfully Made (Psalm 139:14)** - "God did not create me in vain, but He planned the purpose of my life since the beginning. I am a wonderful creation of God who is meant to praise and worship His creator."

3. **I Am Strengthened to Do Anything God Calls Me to Do (Phi-**

lippians 4:13) - "Nothing is difficult for me because Jesus is my strength. He has sent the counselor, the Holy Spirit, to guide me in my weaknesses and hard times."

4. **I Am Never Alone (Hebrews 13:5)** - "God never leaves me because I'm His child. Even when I feel God is not with me, He is still there waiting for me to look at Him and walk with Him."

5. **I Am Loved by God (Romans 8:35-39)** - "My situation, no matter what it is, can't separate me from the everlasting love of God. I can experience God's true love in Christ Jesus."

The truths above help us remember our identity in Christ. However, our quest doesn't end here. It's our responsibility to grasp the complete picture of who we are by finding the treasures hidden in the Word of God. Step in! Identify the voices of truth and live in these life-giving choices. Choose to remember who you are and walk in truth every day.

Ponder:

How deep is my grasp on my true identity in Christ as revealed in His Word? What am I going to do to ensure I walk in my true identity as a believer and not more confusing lies from my enemy?

Scriptures:

2 Corinthians 10:5

We demolish arguments and every pretension that sets itself up against the knowledge of God, and we take captive every thought to make it obedient to Christ.

Ephesians 1:4

For He chose us in Him before the creation of the world to be holy and blameless in His sight.

Prayer:

Lord, let me hear Your voice above the voice of the deceiver. Holy Spirit quicken my heart to the TRUTH. Help me to walk in the identity that You died to give me.

Help me recognize so many lies as the voice of the liar.

CHAPTER 7

Voices of Truth

Where is our solid ground in this shaky, uncertain world? What voices are worth listening to? What behaviors and choices can we count on to be worth making every day?

Several years ago, my daughter and I climbed a mountain together. During our trip, I had a big revelation: it's harder going up and easier coming down. Who would have guessed, right? But we forget this truth all the time in the mountains of our mind. Without conscious effort, we will wander downhill by default. Climbing up mountains toward truth requires a conscious decision every new day.

We can tend to make excuses for accepting lies. Lies are easier, after all. Truth demands excellence and effort from us. We will tell ourselves things like, "I'm justified in my attitude or response because of what *they* said or did." But the fact is, the blame game never works out because in the end, we are ultimately responsible for the choices we make no matter what may have provoked us.

Let's explore some life-giving choices that will ALWAYS be good, no matter what.

We all can choose our focus and our perspective ... a lens through which we see life and events. So, how do you "SEE" your life? Do you see it through the eyes of a victim living in a wretched world? Or do you see through the eyes of trusting a faithful God working all things together? Do you hold a positive or a negative worldview? There are as many answers to the question of perspective as there are people. Some would say that life is like a circus with varied performers. Others say that life is like a symphony with many parts, a puzzle with many pieces, a minefield to navigate. And lastly, some say that life is like a carousel; sometimes you are up and sometimes you are down and sometimes you are just going around and around. Stop and ponder just how you picture life as it truly influences how you live. Your perspective is key to HOW you see life. It shapes your responses to life.

Reframing our perspective allows us to create a different way of looking at a situation, person, circumstance, or relationship. What if you could look at problems, mistakes, or challenges as your greatest resource for learning? Instead of stumbling blocks, you could look at them as stepping stones. The best thing about any mistake is that you get a chance to learn from it. Let the learning begin! What if you believed that everything could add some value to your life, that nothing is wasted? What if you believed that God's promises were actually true and trusted the good Shepherd to work all things together for our good? We cannot control what happens to us, but we can control how we respond, how we frame it and our perspective of it. You can choose your focus at every turn.

The apostle Paul was a great "reframer" of his perspective. His filter of faith and trust allowed him to see differently. When he was in prison in Rome, instead of choosing the perspective of a prisoner, he chose the lens and perspective of preacher and encourager. Read the story in Philippians 1. Remember, as with Paul, you will find whatever you are looking for. Your perspective will lead you. That can be a scary proposition.

Choose to see through the lens of faith. Choose to trust the Trustworthy One and focus on "all that is praiseworthy." God can use your trials to bring about the perfecting of your character. He can turn your stumbling blocks into stepping stones for future usefulness and greater glory. But we must cooperate and allow Him to do so. Choosing His eternal perspective in my life has been a significant game-changer for me.

Ponder:

How can you reframe your perspective to produce greater life-giving results? How could you go from being a victim to being a victor? Name the areas of your life where you need to see from His eternal perspective and purposes.

Scriptures:

Colossians 3:1-2

Since, then, you have been raised with Christ, set your hearts on things above, where Christ is, seated at the right hand of God. Set your minds on things above, not on earthly things.

Philippians 1:12-14

Now I want you to know, brothers and sisters, that what has happened to me has actually served to advance the gospel. As a result, it has become clear throughout the whole palace guard and to everyone else that I am in chains for Christ. And because of my chains, most of the brothers and sisters have become confident in the Lord and dare all the more to proclaim the gospel without fear.

Prayer:

Lord, help me to see through the lens of Your eternal perspective and through the eyes of faith. Help me trust in Your Sovereign ways even when I don't understand. Help me recognize this choice is mine. I choose to focus on Your voice of truth.

Day 2

The Choice of Gratitude

*T*here is transforming power in a grateful heart. It is my greatest antidepressant as I have learned that a grateful heart and an anxious heart cannot reside in the same person. Gratitude has been one of the most significant "game-changers" for my life. I started a gratitude journal years ago when I was drowning, feeling exhausted, overwhelmed, and depressed. With time and consistency, it changed the course of my days and brought my joy back. This was a choice I made. You can make this choice too! You *need* to make this choice too!

Gratitude is the word used to express thankfulness and praise. It refers to the quality of being thankful. Gratitude exemplifies readiness to show appreciation for and to return kindness. Throughout life's trials and blessings, displaying a general attitude of gratitude distinguishes the Christian, but it also makes you a more lovely person to be around! There is so much research about the impact of gratitude on our brain activity and wellness. Practicing gratitude actually increases dopamine in your brain (the stuff that makes you feel good) and encourages your brain to seek more of the same. So, scientifically speaking, the more you are grateful for, the more you will find things to be grateful for.

I believe that the Word commands us to "give thanks in all things" (not for all things) as a drawing card to a deeper place of intimacy and trust. However, at face value, even outside of scripture there are many quotes that teach the power of gratitude. Here are a few for you to ponder:

- "The root of joy is gratefulness ... It is not joy that makes us grateful; it is gratitude that makes us joyful." — Brother David Steindl-Ras

- "Gratitude turns what we have into enough." – Anonymous

- "It is only with gratitude that life becomes rich." – Dietrich Bonhoeffer

- "The more grateful I am, the more beauty I see." – Mary Davis

- "What separates privilege from entitlement is gratitude." – Brené Brown

Besides the power of these quotes, I treasure even more the scripture that tells me to give thanks in all things. That this is God's will for me to be thankful. Scripture also tells us to rejoice always. Rejoicing is an action verb. It is a choice. I know that obedience is rewarded. Gratitude opens our eyes to His blessings. The transforming power of gratitude in my life led to a return of my joy, happiness, and peace. I found a rich calmness to a life lived in gratitude. Join me on this power-filled journey!

Ponder:

How can I develop a greater heart of gratitude? What keeps me from being grateful? Do I need to start a gratitude journal today?

Scriptures:

Colossians 3:17

And whatever you do, whether in word or deed, do it all in the name of the Lord Jesus, giving thanks to God the Father through Him.

1 Thessalonians 5:16-18

Rejoice always, pray continually, give thanks in all circumstances; for this is God's will for you in Christ Jesus.

Prayer:

O Lord, help me to be truly grateful. Open my eyes to see all the blessings that You have given me so that I can live from a heart overflowing with gratitude. Help me recognize this choice is mine. I choose to live with a grateful heart.

Day 3

The Choice of Trust

*T*rust is a confident expectation. Trust, like faith, is not a feeling. It is a choice. I absolutely love referring to Noah Webster's 1828 Dictionary as many of Noah Webster's original word definitions contain references to the King James Bible itself; this was all before it was diluted into our contemporary dictionaries. Literally this is the definition found in that dictionary:

TRUST, noun …

1. Confidence; a reliance or resting of the mind on the integrity, veracity, justice, friendship, or other sound principle of another person.

"He that putteth his trust in the Lord shall be safe" (Proverbs 29:25).

2. He or that which is the ground of confidence.

"O Lord God, thou art my trust from my youth" (Psalms 71:1).

This definition of trust highlights two scriptures about our worthy placement of that trust. I love that "he that putteth his TRUST in the Lord shall be safe" part of the definition above. Safe? Hmmm? In this world we simply cannot put our trust into imperfect humans. There is only One that cannot fail or forsake us. Do we believe that? I do; therefore, I choose to trust Him.

Even though men will inevitably disappoint us, trusting God can also be a challenging choice. It can be nerve-racking, because you eventually need to be okay with not knowing His plans but believing that they are good. This trust choice can be difficult for the control-freak within each of us. The inner part of us that wants to be in-the-know. Trusting a Holy God leaves us not knowing the answers but just trusting the KNOWER of the answers. Do we believe that He is a good, good Father? I do.

We need to realize that trusting God does NOT mean that you believe everything will go the way you want it to. It also doesn't mean that God will explain everything that is going on in your life. As I daily choose trust, I often remind myself to lean not on my own understanding. True trusting brings a letting go as well. It means that no matter what happens, you will turn *to* Him instead of away from Him. It means that whatever we suffer, in the end we trust God will use it for our ultimate good. This brings rest in my trust. Sometimes trust is very hard and is a practice of discipline but trusting God can bring peace and security, because now you are hooked to the Creator, the source of life, power, and prosperity.

The sooner we reconcile His sovereignty and His faithfulness, the sooner we can move on to trust. After trust, we can live in a restful peace. When you trust God, you don't have to understand everything. The Good News: God is just waiting for us to humbly trust Him so He can guide us forward and act with our best interests in mind.

Ponder:

Where do you wrestle with trusting God? Do you really like being in charge of your world and believe that your will, your way is better than His will, His way?

Scriptures:

Proverbs 3:5-6

Trust in the Lord with all your heart and lean not on your own understanding; in all your ways submit to Him, and He will make your paths straight.

Isaiah 26:3

You will keep in perfect peace those whose minds are steadfast, because they trust in You.

Prayer:

Lord, help me to trust You and lean not on my own understanding even whenever my control freak wants to step up and step in. I choose Your Lordship over mine every day. Help me recognize this choice is mine. I choose to trust You.

Day 4

The Choice of Truth

So where is my solid ground in this shaky world? Where is the truth? My solid ground is not found in the opinion of my neighbor nor in my ability to perform well. It is certainly not in the headline news whirling around in our world these weeks! The news speaks of difficult stories, political battles, wars, suffering, unrest, uncertainty, disaster, violence, and evil. This information can leave us feeling overwhelmed with fear or worry, for our children, and for our future. Is this the truth?

Perhaps the most famous verse about truth in the Bible is what Jesus said "... I am the way, and the truth, and the life. No one comes to the Father except through Me" (John 14:6). So Jesus is truth and Jesus is also the Word (John 1:1, 14). He is our guide. As Christians, we believe that every word in the Bible is true. This is the foundation upon which we live our lives. We need to know what the Bible says about truth. We need to hide God's word in our heart to help us to know when we are listening to the Voice of Truth.

Sometimes we just need to turn off our phone, our computers, our TV, and listen to the voice of the One who matters most. His Truth breaks through all that confusion and mess. Let us take every wild, stray, off-track thought captive and make it obedient to the Truth, which can finally set us free. He offers His peace and assurance that no matter what, He still holds all things in His hands. He's not surprised by anything. He's not anxiously pacing Heaven's floors thinking up a Plan B since Plan A didn't work. He reminds us that He's still in control and is the security of our days.

"And He will be the stability of your times, a wealth of salvation, wisdom and knowledge; The fear of the LORD is his treasure" (Isaiah 33:6).

I still love the old hymn about Jesus being the "solid Rock upon which I stand." Jesus is the Rock that won't move or budge. He won't shift this way or that based on popular opinion as His Word is the same yesterday, today, and forever. He won't ever sink or give way to defeat. He is sure and safe, loving and gracious, forgiving and faithful, powerful and strong. His words are the Truth, bringing life and freedom. I am inviting you to rest on the Rock of truth today and always. This is your only solid ground in our shaky world.

Ponder:

Where is your source of truth? Does it provide for your solid ground yesterday, today, and forever? Do you know the Truth?

Scriptures:

Psalm 25:5

Guide me in Your truth and teach me, for You are God my Savior, and my hope is in You all day long.

Psalm 119:160

All Your words are true; all Your righteous laws are eternal.

Prayer:

Lord, help me meditate on Word and know Your truths. I want to stand upon Your solid ground in this crazy, mixed-up, unstable world. Help me recognize this choice is mine.

Day 5

The Choice of Humility

*A*s C.J. Mahaney states in his book *Humility – True Greatness*, "Humility is honestly assessing ourselves in the light of God's holiness and our sinfulness. That's the twin reality that all genuine humility is rooted in: God's holiness and our sinfulness. Without an honest awareness of both these realities, all self-evaluation will be skewed, and we will fail to either understand or practice true humility. We will miss out on experiencing the promise and the pleasures that humility offers." What a powerful truth. I don't want to miss out on any of those promises and pleasures offered by a truly humble heart. Our true size is only revealed as we stand at the foot of the cross and understand the goodness of our God. There is where humility begins.

Another book I read, years ago, was the book *Humility* by Andrew Murray. He suggests that of all the things a Christian could do to be conformed to the image of Christ, we should prioritize seeking humility because therein lies the truth. We must realize that we could not, of our own accord, even produce our own next breath. We are totally dependent on a living God who sustains us for His greater glory through our lives. Just as John 15:5 states, "He is the vine; we are the branches and without Him we can do nothing." How proud can we be of our ability to do nothing? True humility agrees with God's Word. C.J. Mahaney states, "The nearer the soul comes to God, the more His majestic Presence makes it feel its littleness."

The world defines humility as a lowering of oneself in relation to others, a state or the act of being humble, a freedom of pride and arrogance, and having a modest opinion or estimate of one's own worth. True humility, however, is not groveling in front of others, being a doormat, nor is it a sign of weakness. Moses was said to be the meekest man on earth (Num. 12:3) but meekness is not weakness; it's actually strength that is under control. The fact is that "God opposes the proud but gives grace to the humble" (James 4:6).

Whoever is humble is teachable. Humble people are also more likely to learn, to serve, and to not think too highly of themselves. God cannot fill people who are already full of themselves.

Seeking humility may not be the easiest thing to do, but it is definitely where truth lies. The concept of humility takes the load off one's shoulders and brings a grace for greater glory in your life.

Ponder:

Are you strong enough to be humble enough to walk in the truth? It takes wisdom and understanding to clothe yourself in humility and service.

Scriptures:

Isaiah 66:2

These are the ones I look on with favor: those who are humble and contrite in spirit, and who tremble at My word.

Philippians 2:3-4

Do nothing out of selfish ambition or vain conceit. Rather, in humility value others above yourselves, not looking to your own interests but each of you to the interests of the others.

Prayer:

Lord, teach me Your ways of humility in truth. Save me from myself and help me keep You on the throne of my heart. I want to clothe myself in genuine humility and need Your help to do so. Help me recognize this choice is mine.

Day 6

The Choice of Peace

"Peace isn't found in the absence of problems. True Peace is found in the presence of God."

–Craig Groeschel

A dear friend of mine once gave me a placard that read "Choose Peace." Huh? Can I simply just choose peace like I can choose a candy bar? Where is the ever-elusive peace that I can choose? I've spent years pondering how to find peace. How to choose peace. Choosing peace is closely related to the matter of choosing to trust. This is another area of my life that addresses and directly confronts my internal "control freak" nature. My own self upon my own selfish throne.

Scripture says that the LORD offers us His peace and calls us to live as a peacemaker. Isaiah 26 states, "Thou wilt keep him in perfect peace, whose mind is stayed on Thee: because he trusts in Thee. Trust ye in the Lord forever: for in the Lord JEHOVAH is everlasting strength." When trust goes up, our peace goes up. When our trust goes down, we forfeit our peace. So, our peace actually starts with our thoughts and in our minds. We cannot walk in deep peace when our minds are focused on the future, financial problems, or bad news.

Life can often feel so overwhelming or chaotic as the battle for peace always begins in our minds. Juggling a stressful job, multiple relationships, financial woes, and a host of other demands can sometimes be just too much. It's no surprise that we find ourselves internally begging for a moment of peace. WE can be set apart. We can live in a peace that transcends all understanding. But it will only come from an intimate relationship and trust in the Lord. God's deepest desire for every one of us, and for the world at large, is to walk in His peace.

Peace isn't just a feeling or an action you take to make or keep peace. True peace is much deeper than that. Shalom peace is "to take what is broken and restore or reconcile." When life is falling apart all around us, we can choose to step in and experience His shalom peace. As Christians we are called to be agents to minister peace and reconciliation to others. This aligns with the heart of Jesus, who declared, "Blessed are the peacemakers."

Know that the peace that passes understanding is a strong, resolute faith and confidence; no matter what circumstances you encounter, God is faithful, God is good, God will keep you, God will provide for you, and God will bless you. It's a faith that looks past circumstances to the God who works all things for your good and His glory. Peace is living with God's presence in God's perspective and with God's assurance! Even in the middle of the problems.

Ponder:

What inhibits you from choosing to walk in daily peace? How does your life reflect a peace from His presence, His perspective, and His assurance?

Scripture:

Philippians 4:6-7

Do not be anxious about anything, but in every situation, by prayer and petition, with thanksgiving, present your requests to God. And the peace of God, which transcends all understanding, will guard your hearts and your minds in Christ Jesus.

John 14:27

Peace I leave with you; My peace I give you. I do not give to you as the world gives. Do not let your hearts be troubled and do not be afraid.

Prayer:

Lord, help me seek Your peace, which passes all my understanding, in my chaotic world. Help me to trust You more and receive the peace You offer. Help me recognize this choice is mine.

Day 7

The Choice of Grace

Grace is defined as the free, unmerited love and favor of God. What a gift! Since we are all sinners, we all need the free gift of grace. No one is exempt. This is our common ground. Everyone is beautiful (as created by God), yet everyone is messy (as born with a sin condition). #beautifulbutmessy. Upon receiving the gift of grace from God, we should be ambassadors of that living and extending that grace to others.

We cannot know the backstory, the trauma, or the hardships behind other people that we encounter. We cannot know the trials that they have endured. We can simply know that we all need to be loved. Unconditional love can only be extended from a heart of compassion and grace. This is the Father's heart for each of us.

I happen to believe that no one is trying to mess their life up and truly get it wrong. None of us set out to screw up our lives on purpose. I do know that many people are confused, but I have been confused too. I do know that many people can be impatient, but so can I. I do know that people make mistakes, but so do I. Because of these truths, I have made the habit of giving people the benefit of the doubt. It is a powerful life-giving practice! If they didn't really deserve that benefit, then I showed extended grace. If they really did deserve that benefit, then I am glad to have offered such. The world would be a much better place if we all extended grace, wrapped in compassion and forgiveness, for the weaknesses in ourselves and others.

Grace! It is a beautiful act of humility to extend the gift of grace which we have received freely from our Heavenly Father through Christ Jesus. We cannot stand proud as God opposes the proud but gives grace to the humble. The Holy Spirit can give us the strength and the resolve to be gracious in all things. Aren't we all grateful for a "low-maintenance, understanding grace-filled" friend?

Choose to receive the grace of the Father and then extend it to others.

Ponder:

How could understanding the power of grace given help you with a more compassionate heart for yourself and others? In what areas do you need to extend more grace?

Scriptures:

Ephesians 2:8-9

For it is by grace you have been saved, through faith—and this is not from yourselves, it is the gift of God—not by works, so that no one can boast.

James 4:6

But He gives us more grace. That is why Scripture says: "God opposes the proud but shows favor to the humble."

Prayer:

Father, thank You for the gift of Your grace. Help me receive that gift and then, in turn, offer grace to others. I need Your patience, wisdom and understanding in order to do this. Help me recognize this choice is mine.

Day 8
The Choice of Speaking Life

*Y*our thoughts are powerful. "For as a man thinketh so is he ..." (Prov. 23:7).

Your words are powerful. "Life and death are in the power of the tongue" (Prov. 18:21).

Our thoughts and our words determine the direction of our lives. Powerful truth. Pastor Craig of Life Church states, "Our life is always moving in the direction of our strongest thoughts." Our thoughts carry a heavy weightiness. Thoughts lead to beliefs. Beliefs lead to actions. Actions lead to habits. Habits lead to character. Character leads to destiny. Destiny leads to legacy. So it all stems from our thoughts and leads to life impact.

Remember, in "Voices and Choices," we discussed the battlefield going on each day. It starts in our minds and often shows up in our words and our actions. This leads to life and death in our behavior and living. Scripture tells us to fix our thoughts on God's truths and on that which is praiseworthy. If we change our thinking, it can change our lives.

There is proven research in the mind-brain connection. We must pay close attention to the thoughts we allow into our minds as they feed the internal voice and the self-talk we hear. Simply put ... trash in leads to trash out. Very simply put but so very true. We must intentionally take renegade thoughts captive. We must train, discipline, and "set our minds" to receive the life-giving truths found in scripture and put to death whatever thoughts that do not edify and build up. We need to unlock the lies and deception in our thinking. We must speak life-giving truths daily, even back to our own self.

I challenge you to identify renegade, toxic thoughts and replace them with life-giving scriptural antidotes. Then memorize these truths/

scriptures and speak them to yourself daily. You need to think about what you think about. Then you need to hear yourself speak His truths to yourself. Make a list of power-filled scriptural truths and then speak them to yourself and others daily. Write them down. Say them aloud. Speak them out. Repeat. Confess them with your tongue. Make this a new habit and a discipline. Speak life into the environment of those you love and live with. The course of your life depends on it.

Ponder:

What negative, toxic thoughts are weighing your life down? Start paying attention to the positive life-giving words that come out of your own mouth. Speak life into your days.

Scriptures:

Ephesians 4:29

Do not let any unwholesome talk come out of your mouths, but only what is helpful for building others up according to their needs, that it may benefit those who listen.

Proverbs 18:20

From the fruit of their mouth a person's stomach is filled; with the harvest of their lips they are satisfied.

Prayer:

Lord, open my eyes and lead me to Your life-giving truths to replace negative life-sucking thoughts and lies that have plagued me for too long. Help me be the agent for speaking power and life to others. Help me recognize this choice is mine.

Day 9

The Choice of Forgiveness

*A*re you struggling to forgive someone who hurt you? Or are you struggling to forgive yourself? Maybe you are curious about God's forgiveness and even wondering if He could forgive you for something you regret. If you struggle with forgiving others or yourself, then you are not alone.

We are not in charge of the behavior of others, but we are in charge of how we respond. It is only through receiving the grace and forgiveness of God that we can extend the same to others.

Many people have suffered pain and hurt caused by others. This is a harsh reality. But the pain of living with anger, bitterness, resentment, and unforgiveness can poison your soul and destroy you personally. When we forgive others, we are not saying what they did was OK, but we are letting go of their hold on us. Forgiving ourselves and others can be one of the hardest things we face in life, but it will lead to the greatest blessings and freedom as a result.

Despite the prevalence of unforgiveness in our lives, it seems that many of us have a mistaken understanding of forgiveness and its impact, not only spiritually and emotionally, but also physically. In fact, according to John Hopkins Medicine, forgiveness has a huge impact on your own health:

"Whether it's a simple spat with your spouse or long-held resentment toward a family member or friend, unresolved conflict can go deeper than you may realize—it may be affecting your physical health. The good news: Studies have found that the act of forgiveness can reap huge rewards for your health, lowering the risk of heart attack; improving cholesterol levels and sleep; and reducing pain, blood pressure, and levels of anxiety, depression and stress. And research points to an increase in the forgiveness-health connection as you age."

Do not live carrying the heavy burden of unforgiveness any longer. Find freedom through forgiveness. Forgive yourself as well as others. We are all messy. Choose to let go and let God and walk with freedom. Life is too short to spend it angry and upset. "Be kind and compassionate to one another, forgiving each other, just as in Christ God forgave you" (Ephesians 4:32 NIV).

Ponder:

What keeps you from choosing freedom through forgiveness? Have you considered forgiving people even before they hurt you so that you can walk in greater freedom?

Scripture:

Colossians 3:13

Bear with each other and forgive one another if any of you has a grievance against someone. Forgive as the Lord forgave you.

Ephesians 4:31-32

Get rid of all bitterness, rage and anger, brawling and slander, along with every form of malice. Be kind and compassionate to one another, forgiving each other, just as in Christ God forgave you.

Prayer:

Lord, thank You for my complete forgiveness offered through Jesus' death on the cross. Give me Your power to release forgiveness to myself and others. Help me recognize this choice is mine.

Day 10

The Choice of Intimacy with God

We were created to have relationship and fullness in our Creator. Aside from intimacy with our "Knitter and Knower," we are living far below our Christian privilege as believers. However, we have a choice. Sin separated and broke our intimate relationship with our Creator. He loves us so much that He sent His only begotten Son to die for us and restore that broken relationship. But alas, we still have a choice to accept that free gift of our salvation and redemption through the restorative work of His Son, Jesus.

Once we are saved by receiving God's grace and forgiveness through Christ, we still have choices to make. Daily decisions to die to our selfish nature and to live for His purposes and greater glory. This is a decision to walk in a daily relationship and intimacy with Him through His Word, worship, and fellowship with the saints.

Intimacy can be reworded as "into-me-you-see." We need to gaze into the riches of a full-disclosure relationship with our Savior. We need to hide with Him in the secret places. Choosing an intimate, close dependence with God brings peace, wisdom, and strength. Intimacy doesn't bring instant, selfish answers, but it brings a deep and satisfying joy and peace beyond all understanding. It takes time to develop this prized relationship and is worth a million times the effort to seek and search such.

Intimacy with my Lord has brought the greatest satisfaction to my life. He is the only safe love affair of your deepest heart. He loved you enough to die for you and wants to live through you bringing forth your purpose and wholeness.

Are you sick and tired of carrying the heavy yoke of your life? Do you often feel unsure, overwhelmed, or near the end of your rope? This exhausted place is filled with purpose if it will lead you to the all-fulfilling intimacy with your Knitter and Knower, your Savior. He is always beckoning us, but the weight of the world just highlights our need for something more. We are being called back into our first relationship. He loved us, knew us, and numbered our days before there was one of them.

Jump off the fast-paced, exhausting treadmill of your life, and jump into the secret place of intimacy with the Most High. Imagine you're in a slow dance with your greatest Lover and then never step away.

Ponder:

What would it be like to be completely known and completely loved? To be completely safe and secure and alive? What keeps you from investing in this intimate relationship with your Creator?

Scripture:

John 3:16

For God so loved the world that He gave His one and only Son, that whoever believes in Him shall not perish but have eternal life.

Jeremiah 33:3

"Call to me and I will answer you and tell you great and unsearchable things you do not know."

Prayer:

Lord, You knew me before You knit me in my mother's womb. Please draw me back into an intimate, safe relationship with You. I want to abide in the safe secret place with You. Help me recognize this choice is mine.

CHAPTER 8

The Distraction Dilemma

$\mathcal{P}$resident Dwight Eisenhower once reflected, "What is important is seldom urgent and what is urgent is seldom important."

Do you feel like this is ever the case in your life? Do you ever find yourself overwhelmed with so many urgent things that you're unable to commit to the things that matter most? I've known many women who valued quality time with their husband and kids, personal fitness, and meditating on scripture, but find themselves lost in an endless cycle of work, getting kids where they're supposed to go, and keeping up with the house instead.

I mean, I can't get from my bedroom to the laundry room without doing thirteen different distracting things in between. I continually get side-tracked and thrown off course. It feels like I spend my entire life fighting distractions, but God gives us the tools to win!

Have you ever felt like your life has too much "hurry" in it to commit to the things you value most? If so, welcome to the "distraction dilemma" club.

Day 1
Distracted by Definition

*D*aily distractions are a doozy of a dilemma! Oh, my goodness! I have been trying to write this Bible plan for so long, but I keep getting distracted. Well, today is the day! I am drawing a line in the sand. I will not get up from this darn position until I, at least, start this Bible plan which I so desperately need. Do you get easily distracted too? I am convinced that this is part of the arsenal of the enemy to keep us from God's best intentional living. For me, it is a daily battle ground and I remain amazed at just how often I lose the battle to something that distracts me. It is becoming almost laughable at the truth of how distractions can keep me from what is important versus little piddly things that keep me busy. Oh my! I am confident that I am not the only one wrestling with daily distractions.

To distract is to cause one to have difficulty paying attention to something, to attract away from its original focus or to divert. It is from the Latin word "distrahere," which means to draw away or apart. As a Christian, I prioritize building my relationship with God. As a wife, I prioritize investing in my marriage. Since these are two places where I find solid ground, of course the enemy tries to get me as distracted as possible.

Have you heard much about the crisis called "distracted living"? This causes us to miss out on much of our life because we generally aren't paying attention. We are just going from one mindless thing to the next. We are so busy being busy. We are not living INTENTIONAL-LY. Our attention is torn in so many directions that we really don't focus on anything. We know that "distractions" certainly can make learning harder, driving more dangerous, and life less enjoyable. They can be simply exhausting. As a natural part of life, people have dealt with distractions forever. But, with growing social media, comparisons, and busyness, these interruptions seem to be changing with time and increasing in number. As a believer, I hunger to seek His eternal plans for each day but often get distracted by menial things that beckon to get me off-track. Today, start with one focused baby step to live a focused life.

Ponder:

Consider your priorities and consider your distractions. Are you aware of how distracted you may be from the things that really matter to you? How could you prioritize your time better and be less distracted?

Scriptures:

Proverbs 4:25

Let your eyes look straight ahead; fix your gaze directly before you.

Matthew 6:33 (ESV)

But seek first the kingdom of God and His righteousness, and all these things will be added to you.

Prayer:

Lord, open my eyes to the distractions that keep sidelining my priorities. Help me keep the most important things first and be aware of my distractions in doing so. I will choose to prioritize knowing You more.

Day 2

The Blame Game

The blame game started in the Garden of Eden where humanity first came on the scene. Adam blamed Eve. Eve blamed the serpent. And so, it goes! Humans have a huge propensity to blame. This is part of our sin condition. But blaming never leads to successful living. Let's be honest. We all have pointed the finger at someone at some point in our lives. So, whenever I get distracted or off course in my day, who am I to blame? Where is my scapegoat for my distracted living? I am thinking that I need to have a long talk with the lady that I see in the mirror every morning! The one that always "sits in my chair." As we grow in Christ, we should not be blaming others for our mistakes, but instead take full responsibility for our own actions. This can be very humbling. After taking a deep breath, I need to realize that it is up to me to be in charge of me. Ugh! Since I cannot judge or change others' behavior, I have to square up with the fact that it is up to me to change my responses. I need to invite the Holy Spirit to help me make wise daily choices. The Word says that He will give me strength whenever I am weak.

Have you ever heard of boundaries? The idea of making decisions about what you will or won't let impact your life. Clear boundaries are essential to a healthy and productive lifestyle. Whenever I have to go to work, I simply don't get distracted by things that beg my attention otherwise. This is an easy boundary to learn. Other boundaries can be more difficult. But in the end, I am in charge of me and how I respond to outside stimulus. I am in charge of the intentionality of my days. This is an internal battle and an idea worth deep contemplation. Do not be discouraged. Invite the Holy Spirit in to help you and strengthen you each day.

Now is the time to start taking greater personal responsibility for the outcome of your days. Make wise choices. Set wise boundaries. Look in the mirror and agree with yourself that today you will not be distracted from those things that are most important to you. I believe in you.

Ponder:

Consider the priorities of your days. Do you blame others for your distracted living or inability to get things done? Where could you take more responsibility for the outcome of your daily choices?

Scriptures:

Romans 2:1-3

You, therefore, have no excuse, you who pass judgment on someone else, for at whatever point you judge another, you are condemning yourself, because you who pass judgment do the same things. Now we know that God's judgment against those who do such things is based on truth. So when you, a mere human being, pass judgment on them and yet do the same things, do you think you will escape God's judgment?

Isaiah 41:10

So do not fear, for I am with you; do not be dismayed, for I am your God. I will strengthen you and help you; I will uphold you with My righteous right hand.

Prayer:

Lord, I do not want to blame others for the end result of my life. I need You desperately. Help me prioritize my days, take personal responsibility, and live Your best life for me. I will choose to prioritize knowing You more.

---

*B*elow is a story that's been circulating for a while. I believe it holds a very important message regarding appropriately setting priorities in our lives and minimizing distractions.

"A professor of philosophy stood before his class with some items in front of him. When the class began, wordlessly he picked up a large empty mayonnaise jar and proceeded to fill it with rocks about two inches in diameter. He then asked the students if the jar was full.

They agreed that it was full.

So, the professor then picked up a box of pebbles and poured them into the jar. He shook the jar lightly and watched as the pebbles rolled into the open areas between the rocks. The professor then asked the students again if the jar was full.

They chuckled and agreed that it was indeed full this time.

Then the professor picked up a box of sand and poured it into the jar. The sand filled the remaining open areas of the jar.

'Now,' said the professor, 'I want you to recognize that this jar signifies your life. The rocks are the truly important things, such as family, health, and relationships. If all else was lost and only the rocks remained, your life would still be meaningful. The pebbles are the other things that matter in your life, such as work or school. The sand signifies the remaining 'small stuff' and material possessions.'

If you put sand into the jar first, there is no room for the rocks or the pebbles. The same can be applied to your lives. If you spend all your time and energy on the small stuff, you will never have room for the things that are truly important."

Many people have really made a mess of their lives by having the wrong priorities in life. We all must become great managers of our time and prioritize the things that are most important in our lives. As Andy Stanley states, "We don't drift in good directions. We discipline and prioritize ourselves there." We must learn to number and take account for our days. Pay attention to and note the things in life that are critical to your happiness and well-being. Each day must be valued as a gift given with a new slate. Then we can fill in our extra time with other, less significant things. I challenge you now to make a list of your *larger stones* (most valued things in life), your *pebble-sized stones* (other important things), and then *your sand grains* (small stuff and material possessions). Take care of the rocks first – things that really matter. Set your priorities. Don't get too distracted. The rest is just sand.

Ponder:

Consider the weight of your priorities. Measure them in view of your daily choices. Decide if you live by the priorities of the "stones, pebbles, and sand" values that you have defined for your life.

Scriptures:

Luke 12:29-31

And do not set your heart on what you will eat or drink; do not worry about it. For the pagan world runs after all such things, and your Father knows that you need them. But seek His kingdom, and these things will be given to you as well.

Psalm 90:12

Teach us to number our days, that we may gain a heart of wisdom.

Prayer:

Lord, please help me in evaluating Your priorities and purposes for my life. I invite You to enter into my daily decisions to live by design. I will choose to prioritize knowing You more.

Day 4

Busyness

*O*ne of our greatest distractions is simply "BUSYNESS." Often, we have this illusion of self-importance based on a busy life. Many times, busyness and achievement can be a cover up for other issues in our lives.

Let me tell you a story about the devil having a garage sale, selling his "tools." One of the items he was selling was very expensive. When inquired about such an expensive item, the devil replied, "Oh, that item has such a high price because it is one of my most valuable tools." Upon further inquiry, the devil explained, "I call this tool BUSYNESS as I can keep everyone so distracted and off course/purpose ... and yet, they never really know it."

Ugh! This is the story of my life. Whether my calendar is full, or there are other important issues beckoning, I can simply stay busy almost doing nothing of great importance. I hate this in myself. Focus has been a battle all of my life. Years and years ago, I would likely have been diagnosed "ADHD" or maybe more rightfully "ADDDEFGH." Easily distractible. Often busying myself with so many unimportant things that ended up crowding out time for the important things. Totally getting sidetracked, yet feeling so important because I was simply busy!

Reflecting on the Bible story about Mary and Martha, I often feel very convicted about my priorities. Martha busied herself with tasks while Mary sat at the feet of Jesus to worship Him. Martha "was distracted." Jesus admonished Martha that Mary was doing the most important thing. I do realize that we have works to do here on earth, but the overarching point of this story, to me, questions whether I am living out of a performance-based mentality or whether I am living out of my intimate relationship with my Lord. Do I live FOR Him on my ever-running performance treadmill? Or do I live FROM Him out of a deep, motivated relationship with Him? Christ in me, through me, and from me is my only true hope of glory (Col. 1:27).

The Bible says that busyness can lead to doubt and spiritual disconnection from God. In Psalm 46:10 there is a direct link between being still and knowing that God truly is God. If we are too busy for God, our stillness before the Lord will vanish, along with our peace of mind. The sinful nature, the world, and Satan thrive when we are too busy for God.

Trust God with your schedule, making the most of every opportunity. Don't underestimate the value of seeking His wisdom. Wisdom is a HUGE time saver and success maker! Think twice before committing to something. Pause, pray, and consider! Leave some margin in your life for miracles to happen.

Ponder:

Are you too busy being just busy, or are you busy with those most important things that are a priority for you? How can you adjust your days to usher in a more calming pace for living?

Scriptures:

1 Peter 5:8

Be alert and of sober mind. Your enemy the devil prowls around like a roaring lion looking for someone to devour.

Luke 10:41-42

"Martha, Martha," the Lord answered, "you are worried and upset about many things, but few things are needed—or indeed only one. Mary has chosen what is better, and it will not be taken away from her."

Prayer:

Oh Lord! Please keep me from the empty pursuit of a busy life all the while squeezing out a purpose-filled life. Help me be aware of just how too much "busyness" can be the enemy's tool for distracted living. I will choose to prioritize knowing You more.

Day 5

Identifying Distractions

*A*re you like me? Days can often just disappear as they fly by like a fast-moving train. Whether we are at a job in our workplace or ministering to family members in our households, most of us are plenty busy. Some of us serve in outside ministries as well.

Living out one distracted day at a time, we can end up with a life that is totally off course. Inch by inch, we can end up a mile away from our heart's intentions. Life is not a dress rehearsal. We do not get to live this day over again. We need to identify distracting culprits and recognize their impact on our days. A couple of life's greatest distractions include television and social media. More subtle distractions can show up as fear, worry, comparison, and depression. Even though real, these nuances certainly can take our energy away.

I can get distracted by piddly little things, like checking my cell phone, doing the dishes or the laundry. All these things are necessary but can simply be distractions. It is also easy to waste energy being distracted by things that we cannot even control, like the news, the weather, or the traffic. We need to be cognizant of time wasted by things beyond our control.

Here are a few things that we don't generally consider as distractions, but they might be.

#1 – Pleasure/Ease – I can be deterred by any fun thing. We must consider if we are living for shallow pleasures versus what is important. Just ensure you balance your times of refreshment.

#2 – Pride – Pride can distract us into diversions and side-track our daily intentions. Often, we follow wherever our ego leads us.

#3 – Procrastination – Frequently, we KNOW the right decision that needs to be made … but because it may be tough to do so, we delay it. We can exhaust ourselves putting off something that could easily be done. Don't waste your time procrastinating.

#4 – People – Pleasing people can be exhausting and often get us off-track. Someone is always going to not like what you do, who you are, and what you stand for (See Galatians 1:10). Live for the audience of ONE.

#5 – Performance – The performance treadmill keeps many of us off focus. We have this overriding voice wooing us to simply try harder and harder, work harder and harder … thus establishing an exhausting pace of performance.

#6 – Problems – We can't view problems as God's punishment … but rather we must view them as God's preparation! Reframing our problems as challenges can be a stepping stone to greater maturing and opportunity.

#7 – Passion – Your passion can lead towards purpose, but an overriding or misguided passion can be a distraction when we idolize it and use it to run over people or to dominate your scheduled priorities.

Ponder:

What "good things" in your life are still keeping you distracted from the "greater things?" Consider if you are allowing the things that you want NOW to distract you from the things that you want MOST.

Scriptures:

Matthew 6:34

Therefore do not worry about tomorrow, for tomorrow will worry about itself. Each day has enough trouble of its own.

1 Peter 5:8

Be alert and of sober mind. Your enemy the devil prowls around like a roaring lion looking for someone to devour.

Prayer:

Lord, help keep me focused on the most important things for today. Help me live one undistracted day at a time only allowing for Your divine interruptions. I will choose to prioritize knowing You more.

Day 6

Intentional Living

So how do we resolve our distraction dilemma? Am I the only one with this problem? Are the rest of you totally focused and able to accomplish all your priorities each day? Here are a few helpful steps we can take toward less distractions and more intentional living:

1. Start each day aligning with our God, our priorities, and our purposes. Maybe even start this at bedtime, the night before. Never feel guilty about spending pleasing time with the Lord, your Creator. He can lead, guide, direct, and prioritize our steps. Consider writing down those items that simply MUST get accomplished. From there we need to act with conviction and intention, limiting distractions and diversions. This takes intentionality in thinking through your daily choices. The more we are aware of this dilemma the more we can manage it. Invite the Holy Spirit into this process and ask the Spirit to lead, guide, and direct your days. Seek His wisdom. Your days are fleeting. Let's be intentional, yet flexible!

2. Consider fasting from technology and social media for a time period. You may even need to announce to others that you are doing so. The "advancement" of social media can imprison all of us in a distracted life. The new downtime can aid us in reevaluating and reprioritizing our lives. After we spend some time limiting TV and social media, we come to realize just what a distraction they actually were. Not only can social media infringe on our schedule, it can even define who we are. In truth, our souls just need a break from the constant bombardment of information that often lead to comparisons and negativity. Should you even consider, on a Saturday or Sunday, handing your cell phone, and other devices, over to a friend or loved-one? Take a deep breath. Read a book. Go for a walk. Reflect on who you are and who you want to be ... especially when no one is watching. Limiting TV/social media distractions can help you reframe your choices. We need to think differently

about our devices so that we can live differently and less distracted.

3. Be vigilant about identifying and eliminating other "time wasters." Don't fall into the trap of being constantly on the go. Avoid doing meaningless work by staying in constant prayerful communication with God. Stop and consider where you are losing precious time to irrelevant or unimportant things. Consider logging your time for a period. Notice time wasters that infringe on your productivity and priorities. Could you limit phone calls to shorter conversations? Could you multitask a few items together to save valuable time?

Consider the wisdom of evaluating your life in terms of true distractions. May I suggest that we never pack our lives so tightly that we leave no room for a miracle to show up through a Divine Interruption. Leave space for God to show up and show off. Live intentionally and less distracted.

Ponder:

What time wasters could I eliminate that don't bring a rich value exchange for my time today? How can I live more intentionally?

Scriptures:

Psalm 32:8

I will instruct you and teach you in the way you should go; I will counsel you with My eye upon you.

James 1:5

If any of you lacks wisdom, you should ask God, who gives generously to all without finding fault, and it will be given to you.

Prayer:

Lord, I know that each day is a gift. Let me live each day intentionally. I don't want to live so distracted that I miss your best for my life. I need you, Lord! I will choose to prioritize knowing You more.

CHAPTER 9

The Gift in You

Why are we here? Why did God make us? What's the point of all this?

All the time, we wonder if there is a purpose for why we are here and what kind of value we could possibly have in such a grand universe. The truth is kind of amazing, really: God made YOU! He handcrafted you, dreamed of you, and breathed Himself into you. Just imagine the kind of worth and value the Creator places on you! It's then our responsibility to remember our true identity and purpose.

Scripture promises that God has put a world-changing gift within every human being, but that same gift is what the enemy fights to keep hidden. I believe that we Christians live so very far below our Christian privilege. To find the gift in me, I chose to disregard the lies from the devil and start weighing what I'm good at, what I love, what my values are, and what my strengths are. Once I discovered my gifts, I also learned that God implanted them to serve others in the body of Christ. Gifts are given to give away in service to others. You cannot outgive the Gift-Giver! Let's find your sweet spot and use it to live for His greater glory.

If you want to walk in the power of fully knowing your identity and purpose, join me on this chapter! There is a gift in you!

Day 1

Knitted and Known

*B*efore God invaded eternity with the idea of "TIME," He existed. Nothing else. Then God started creating everything as described in Genesis 1. Finally, in His greatest work, He created man. He said this creation was "very good."

Scripture says that before we lived even one day, He knew us. He knit us in our mother's womb. Knitting is intricate handwork, but, for God, it was a "fearfully and wonderfully made" handiwork. No creator creates anything without some intention to the design and the same is true for our Creator Father. Wrapping our mind around being personally and intentionally knitted and known by a perfect Holy Creator God, leaves us humbly asking, "But why?"

So, what is our Designer's purpose? This question has been asked across generations by millions.

Each of us is a unique creation made in the image of a Holy God. No two humans are alike.

Each of us is gifted with strengths, personality, and giftings. Then, on top of that, we are signed with our own personal thumbprint. We are gifted so that we can serve others with our gifts. Each unique. Each individual. He brings forth His purposes for our lives through this principle of individuality.

The personal "knitting" suggests that we are created ON purpose, FOR purpose, and WITH purpose. No one knits something accidentally! When a knitter knits, it is with a plan in mind. A vision. There is a plan for each of our matchless lives. The devil does not want us to believe this or pursue this truth.

Since I was deliberately created by a Creator, what was my designed purpose and calling? Do I know it? Could I miss it? Why was I created in this time of world history? These questions have always burdened my mind. They keep me searching and open for the "Knitter's" intent. Can we discover that intent or purpose? Tragically, can we completely miss it? If all creation beckons us to the heart of God, then let's respond and seek to live out our assignments. Since life is not a dress rehearsal, it would be a shame to miss it! Let's study His Word to gain greater confidence as to the gift within each of us since we were knitted and known for such a time as this.

Ponder:

Ponder your creation from the heart of our Creator. Could you be an accident if you were intentionally KNITTED in your mother's womb? What are His intentions for your life?

Scriptures:

John 1:3

Through Him all things were made; without Him nothing was made that has been made.

Psalm 139:13-14

For You created my inmost being, You knit me together in my mother's womb. I praise You because I am fearfully and wonderfully made; Your works are wonderful; I know that full well.

Prayer:

Lord, teach me Your purposes in knitting me fearfully and wonderfully in my mother's womb. I don't want to miss a thing. I want to live in the fulfillment of Your intentional assignment for my life. Thank You Lord for the gift in me specifically designed to serve others.

Day 2

Assigned for Such a Time

"For such a time as this" is a phrase tossed around frequently, often without much thought to the original meaning or context. It can mean special, chosen, or set apart. Many people even quote Mordecai's rebuke to Esther as a life-verse representing power and favor.

But what did this phrase really mean?

In His creation, everything and everyone plays such a significant role in the fulfillment of God's purpose for men and nations. We were not just created haphazardly but in a specific family, in a specific nation, and in a specific decade of time. None of us chose our parents, our siblings, our birth-cities, or the decade of our birth.

When we look at the life of Esther throughout the book titled in her name, this phrase actually refers to Esther being scolded for her self-indulgent, self-preserving mindset. She was living for her own agenda versus for the Lord's greater purposes. It is so easy to be self-centered. It is so easy to live an indulgent lifestyle. However, I don't want to miss His grander purposes for my life because I am wrapped up in my own agenda. Do you?

"For such a time as this": These words beckon us to consider the "Larger Story" of purpose and intention for our lives. Maybe we all need to be reminded of our destiny, set aside our own interests, and yield to the greater work at hand. This requires a heart to look outward for serving others, versus looking inward to serve ourselves. This is a choice set before us.

God has blessed each of us. He has opened doors and opportunities to optimize His kingdom purposes. He didn't place you or me where we are, so we could waste our days on social media and selfish endeavors He's placed us wherever we are with intention for our gift of good works. Are we participating by design or are we haphazardly wasting our days?

We need to view our lives through the lens of "such a time as this" in order to activate greater awareness of the possibilities of ministry right in front of us.

Submitting to the influence of the indwelling Holy Spirit will aid our understanding and insight into His purposes. Ask for this guidance and then respond in service. See a need? If possible, meet the need. Considering the potential impact that one life can make on another, we must question our availability for usefulness. When God calls, He is serious. We need to live aware and ready to yield to the greater work at hand. Oftentimes. this is simply a ministry to your neighbor on your right and on your left … for such a time as this.

Ponder

What are some ways the Lord is asking you to sacrifice on behalf of His purpose of serving others? What's one step you can take to move more fully into His calling for such a time as this?

Scripture:

Esther 4:13-14 (NASB)

Then Mordecai told them to reply to Esther, "Do not imagine that you in the king's palace can escape any more than all the Jews. For if you remain silent at this time, relief and deliverance will arise for the Jews from another place and you and your father's house will perish. And who knows whether you have not attained royalty for such a time as this?"

Proverbs 16:4a (NASB)

The LORD has made everything for its own purpose.

Prayer:

Lord, turn my heart and my mind toward You and toward the role You have chosen for me *"for such a time as this."* Help me to put Your will and Your purpose ahead of my own. I humbly bow before You and ask for Your guidance, as well as Your courage to live out the calling I've been given. Thank You Lord for the gift in me specifically designed to serve others.

Day 3

Uniquely and Beautifully You

*O*nly you can be you. No one else is coming to be you. You are gifted to be uniquely and beautifully you … SO THAT God's generosity can flow through you into service to others!

First Corinthians 12 addresses each member of the body of Christ as uniquely gifted. This chapter uses human anatomy as a powerful picture to illustrate how we are designed to function together, each part different but equally important and needed. "Now there are varieties of gifts, but the same Spirit. And there are varieties of ministries, and the same Lord. There are varieties of effects, but the same God who works all things in all persons. But to each one is given the manifestation of the Spirit for the common good" (1 Corinthians 12:4-7 NASB). The body of Christ needs you and your unique gifting to function as it should.

Secondly, you have a unique personality temperament. Across the years there have been many personality assessments each with their own style of descriptive analysis. Many of us are introverts while others are extroverts. Many of us are task-oriented while others are people-oriented. Some assessments go into layers and layers of character descriptions while others are more simplified.

Thirdly, you have been uniquely equipped with certain strengths or skill sets. Strength-finder assessments are a huge buzz-word in the workplace these days. Employees function better and have increased job satisfaction when operating in areas of their strengths. Team-building utilizes the individual strengths of each team member to make the team stronger and more productive as a whole. We must all remember that "strengths overused can become a weakness."

One great way to see what God has planned for your life is to look at the skills that you have been blessed with to use for His glory. If

God has gifted you musically, serve Him on the church worship team or other avenue to musically bless others. Do you like public speaking? Maybe God could be calling you to be a preacher. Do you like hands-on activities? Maybe consider missions or becoming a caretaker of the church. If you aren't already involved in your church, please consider the skills you have been given by God and see how you can serve and benefit His kingdom. Serving others can be deeply satisfying to the human heart.

Fourthly, we each have specific "core values." These are the guiding principles that pilot our decisions and behaviors. Core values can help us (or our businesses) as a filter to determine if we are on the right path to fulfilling personal or business goals. They create an unwavering and unchanging guide. Core values are revealed by the way that we live. They are principles that characterize our lives. Some examples of core values are teamwork, compassion, integrity, missions, family, positivity, faith, endurance, accountability, enthusiasm, etc.

We simply cannot compare our giftings with those of others. We are all needed and valuable. Feel free to be you, uniquely you, but be the very BEST YOU.

Ponder:

Consider your own unique gifts and strengths. You are a unique part of a larger body of usefulness and purpose. How can you offer your gifts to serve others?

Scripture:

1 Peter 4:10

Each of you should use whatever gift you have received to serve others, as faithful stewards of God's grace in its various forms.

1 Corinthians 12:4-11 (NASB)

Now there are varieties of gifts, but the same Spirit. And there are varieties of ministries, and the same Lord. There are varieties of effects, but the same God who works all things in all persons. But to each one is given the manifestation of the Spirit for the common good. For to one is given the word of wisdom through the Spirit, and to another the word of knowledge according to the same Spirit; to another faith by the same Spirit, and to another gifts of healing by the one Spirit, and to another the effecting of miracles, and to another prophecy, and to another the distinguishing of spirits, to another various kinds of tongues, and to another the interpretation of tongues. But one and the same Spirit works all these things, distributing to each one individually just as He wills.

Prayer

Lord, I pray for greater revelation as to how to use my intentional gifts to serve Your story and purposes. Open my eyes and help me be mindful of my unique value and my potential contributions to serve others well. Thank You Lord for the gift in me specifically designed to serve others.

Day 4

Redeeming Your Past

So, what about those of us who have screwed up our pasts which are littered with brokenness, shame, and poor choices? We believe that our story isn't worth telling. Is there a GIFT in us? Since our Creator is also our Redeemer (Eph. 1:7) and Restorer (Joel 2:25-26), we can live with the real hope of renewed purpose even from the most traumatic pasts. It is life-giving to know and to trust that He makes all things new (Rev 21:5), and He works all things together for His greater good (Rom. 8:28). This is our hope and our solid ground!

You are not defined by your past, but your past can prepare you for future usefulness. The good news is that we can trust Him to use our entire past for redemptive purposes in our future. Allowing God to redeem our past is a critical choice that we all have to make. Since God is the perfect steward, and He does not waste a thing. All things CAN be used for future good IF we allow Him to do the redeeming and restoring work. He is not intimidated by things that threaten us. He is working to bring good – to achieve glory – from our pasts and our pains. However, it is up to us to ASK for it and to YIELD to this work. He can heal our broken places as well as our broken hearts. He desires to bring "purpose from our pain" and "ministry from our misery." These redemptive stories are our unique gift to give the world. They are our testimony of His faithfulness. As He comforts us, we are to comfort others. He will take the ashes of our past and turn them into crowns of beauty ... beauty from ashes.

Our redeemed lives can be viewed as a beautiful tapestry woven with purpose and design. It may look messy from one point of view (the back of the tapestry), but, ultimately, our yielded life can be His creative work on the "front side." The dark threads of our trials and brokenness add dimension and beauty to our story. Yield and invite Him to the redemptive work from your past. Let Him "work things together for the good of those that love Him and are called according to His purpose."

Invite God to redeem your past. It is a gift that you can give to yourself and others. The storyline of your life is rich with valuable lessons that can point to how to love Him, love ourselves and others more. Let the redeeming work begin!

Ponder

How can you allow the Lord to bring a redeeming purpose from your past pains and heartbreak? Your own personal redemption story is your gift to this world.

Scripture:

Ephesians 1:7

In Him we have redemption through His blood, the forgiveness of sins, according to the riches of His grace

Joel 2:25-26

"I will repay you for the years the locusts have eaten—the great locust and the young locust, the other locusts and the locust swarm—My great army that I sent among you. You will have plenty to eat, until you are full, and you will praise the name of the Lord your God, who has worked wonders for you; never again will my people be shamed."

Prayer

Lord, open my eyes to where You want to use the pains of my past for your future purposes and glory. As You have comforted me, let me be the hands and feet of comfort for others. Help me to realize the opportunities hidden in my past for greater usefulness. Thank You Lord for the gift in me specifically designed to serve others.

Day 5
Your Story for Greater Glory

God is the author of history or His-Story. He is carrying out His plan on earth. HE is Sovereign over His creation. He works in significant and (seemingly) insignificant events to accomplish His purposes for you. He is consistently unfolding His story throughout each life that He created.

You are a unique part of His larger story. No one can tell your story for the greater glory like you. When it comes to sharing Jesus with the world, there are simply some things that ONLY you can do. Not your pastor. Not your mother. There is no one coming behind you to do the work that ONLY you can do. You are a gift. Others can't say it like you or do it like you. No one else can tell your story or share about what Jesus has done FOR YOU, like you. Your story of redemption can minister to others as a gift, wrapped in you. This is significant work! You! Nothing you ever do through the indwelling power of Christ is ever insignificant.

Everyone reckons with their past. Most have times of heartbreak and celebration—the "peaks and the pits," so to speak. As we review the timeline of our lives, we can see rich and valuable lessons that add color to our story. Christians can take courage that He is working everything for our good even IN the most difficult life situations. Ephesians 2:10 tells us that we were created as His handiwork (masterpiece) and assigned good works that were prepared FOR US! Your story, your uniqueness, and individuality are all a gift! Don't miss this. Don't let the enemy rob you of this truth. You are one-of-a-kind and signed with a thumbprint all your own and a story all your own.

Instead of just living in the small story of our own lives, we have the opportunity to see our story as a contributing part of the "Greater Story." We are a significant and needed part of the full Body of Christ. We can share our story of His faithfulness to redeem and restore our past. The conversation of telling our redemptive stories is our gift to love God and love others well.

God is always at work. Would you join Him by allowing Him to bring forth His purposes and plans through the significance of your life? What a privilege it is for us. What a gift to give! The gift in you! Your story for His greater glory.

Ponder:

How am I living in His larger story versus my self-centered smaller story? Do I realize the significance of sharing the gift inside of me? My story for His greater glory.

Scripture:

Philippians 2:13

For it is God who works in you to will and to act in order to fulfill His good purpose.

Romans 8:28

And we know that in all things God works for the good of those who love Him, who have been called according to His purpose.

Prayer

Lord, I want to join into your purposes for the gift of my life. Help me walk in your redemptive ways so that I can love others as You have loved me. I yield to your work in my story for Your glory! Thank You Lord for the gift in me specifically designed to serve others.

CHAPTER 10

Speaking Life

What's your favorite thing someone's told you this week, month, or year? Maybe it's a small thing like, "You're the best momma ever!" or "I love you" or "Girl, you make the best smoothies *ever!*" Whatever it is, do you notice how even the smallest words of love and encouragement can drastically impact you?

We must consider our words. Do you breathe life in so that you can breathe life out or do you wallow in draining words of death? Speak life to yourself and others.

Words have an indescribable power. How are you wielding it?

Day 1

The Power of the Tongue

*L*ife and death are harnessed in the power of our tongue. Do we believe this? Even though the tongue is a small thing, it can make grand speeches. A tiny spark can set a great forest on fire. The rudder of a ship is another small thing that can direct the course of a large vessel. Among all the parts of our body, the tongue is the most powerful and can set your world on fire or breathe life into a weary soul. You choose.

The Word tells us that our words can be like a scorching fire, separating close friends, stirring up anger, and providing the folly of fools. In contrast, the Word also says that our tongue can speak words that bring life … words like apples of gold, life-giving water, or honey to the soul. Our words have impact, for good or ill.

Our tongue and its power to use words is a unique and influential gift from God. When we read the book of Proverbs, we must notice that verse upon verse about the power of our words keep jumping off the page. Proverbs 12:6 teaches that our words have the power to destroy and the power to build up. Are we using the words from our tongue to build up people or destroy others? Who's in charge of your tongue? Who can we blame when hurtful things come tumbling out of our mouths? It is imperative that we make a conscious decision to control the output of our own tongues.

Since our powerful, positive, and beautiful words can heal and uplift, we must be lavish in these words. When spoken with truth, our words have the ability to change lives. Stop and think about how you communicate. Do your words encourage people to achieve greatness? Do your words support and help someone who is suffering? Do your words nurture, nourish, and inspire your own children?

Sadly, emotions like hatred, fear, anger, doubt, frustration, and resentment can be expressed and fueled by words as well. Whether words are written or spoken, they have the power to break and destroy healthy environments, as well as relationships.

Years ago, I accepted the challenge presented in Ephesians 4:29 which states, "Do not let any unwholesome talk come out of your mouths, but only what is helpful for building others up according to their needs, that it may benefit those who listen." What a powerful directive. This would be a project in taming my tongue. I have witnessed the barren desert of hurtful words. I was excited to go on this new life-giving adventure. I wanted to speak life into my world, starting with my own tongue.

Since our tongue wields the mighty power for life or for death, we must be mindful about what we say and how we say it. Be wise! Consider your words. Your words can change everything!

Ponder:

Small. Quick. Easy. Consider the impact of your words. How can you speak more life-giving truths and not words that destroy? Ponder new ways to choose to build others with your words.

Scripture:

Proverbs 18:21

The tongue has the power of life and death, and those who love it will eat its fruit.

James 3:5-6 NLT

... The tongue is a small thing that makes grand speeches. But a tiny spark can set a great forest on fire. And among all the parts of the body, the tongue is a flame of fire. It is a whole world of wickedness, corrupting your entire body. It can set your whole life on fire, for it is set on fire by hell itself.

Prayer:

Lord, please help me to become super aware of the power in my tongue and my chosen words. Help me to speak life and not death, to build-up and not tear down. I will choose to speak life-giving words every day.

Day 2
Think About What You Think About

*O*ur thoughts matter. There is life-giving power in our thoughts. Proverbs 23:7 (KJV) states, "For as a man thinketh in his heart, so is he." Our thoughts matter as out of the abundance of our thoughts flow our words. The thoughts and inclinations of our heart shape the reality of who we are. They shape our thinking which will ultimately shape our words and therefore, our actions. What we say matters but what we think matters even more. Scripture tells us to think about, even dwell on, that which is praiseworthy. Do we actually invest in and prioritize this obedience?

There are many books written that examine how our words are simply the vehicles that convey our thoughts and emotions. What we put in our mind impacts what you think. Does "trash in equal trash out?" If so, our thoughts should be considered our highest priority, especially since the health and welfare of our lives are the by-product. Our enemy wants our minds filled with all sorts of trash and vain imaginations. Let's think about what we think about.

Neuro linguistic programming acknowledges the fundamental connection between the brain (*neuro*) with our thoughts, language (*linguistic*) as our words, and our internal and external behaviors or actions (*programming*). This school of thought considers the practical application of thought awareness as it relates to positive healthy living.

Since we find what we are looking for, we have to really think about what we are looking at. As the story goes … there was a vulture and a hummingbird flying over the same desert. The vulture was looking for death and decay to eat on. The vulture found death and decay. By contrast, the hummingbird was looking for life in the nectar of a flower. The hummingbird found life. They both found what they were looking for. Be very careful what you look for, what you think about, and what you let go into the windows of your mind. For out of the abundance of our thoughts our words flow.

Second Corinthians 10:5 tells us that we are to "demolish arguments and every pretension that sets itself up against the knowledge of God and take captive every thought to make it obedient to Christ." It is possible to live a life aware of our thoughts and take them captive! God gave us the Holy Spirit to empower us to do so. Taking your thoughts captive simply means gaining control over what you think about yourself and life.

When we dwell on all our blessings, the character of our loving God and Father, and all His beauty seen in nature, then we live from those settling truths. However, whenever we think about what we don't have and what is wrong with our world, we can struggle with depression and anxiety. There is a battlefield in your mind. Your life will always move in the direction of your strongest thoughts. So, arm your mind and thoughts with life-giving truth!

Ponder:

Take time to consider your thoughts throughout the day. Are they life-giving and positive? Are they negative? What input establishes your thoughts each day?

Scripture:

Psalm 19:14

May these words of my mouth and this meditation of my heart be pleasing in Your sight, Lord, my Rock and my Redeemer.

2 Corinthians 10:5

We demolish arguments and every pretension that sets itself up against the knowledge of God, and we take captive every thought to make it obedient to Christ.

Prayer:

Lord, help me be cognizant of my thoughts as they lead to my words. I want life-giving thoughts to lead my tongue to life-giving words. I need Your Word of Truth to dwell in my thoughts. Help me take every thought captive that doesn't align with Your truths. I will choose to speak life-giving words every day.

Day 3

Choosing to Speak Life

*C*hoose your words carefully. What we say matters. Words are singularly the most powerful force available to humanity. We can choose to use this power constructively, building up others, or destructively, tearing them down. It only takes a few words to hurt someone. And those wounds may heal but they leave scars that never disappear. Our words have enormous power with the ability to help or to harm, to heal or to hurt, to lift or to destroy, to build up or to tear down, to offend or to befriend, to affirm or to alienate, to comfort or to criticize.

The words spoken in our homes have a profound and an astounding impact for future health and well-being. Parents can lash out with tongues that slice and dice and totally devastate their children. And children can explode at their parents with words that level the entire family like a bomb. When we react and then respond to a situation with really destructive words, the implications can be overwhelming and soul-destroying for the recipient. It's very easy to put voice to our feelings and thoughts; however, it takes control, strength, and absolute integrity to express ourselves in a positive way no matter the situation. Stop and take a breath before you speak, especially when you are stressed. As parents, we need to speak life into our children from the day they are born.

Spouses must consider the power in their words to one another. Our jobs, the world news, children, and life itself are often wearing. We need to build our marriages and our homes with positive, uplifting encouragement that comes from a life-giving faith and not from trauma, anxiety, or fear.

Joyce Landorf Heatherley wrote a book called *Balcony People*. "Some people are in the 'balcony' of your life, cheering you on, energizing you with their affirmation. Others are in your 'basement' doing exactly the opposite. This book is about being a *balcony person.*" Are you a balcony person? Or a basement person?

Satan's schemes to get us to underestimate the power of our words. Since his nature is to destroy, he works constantly to get your words flowing in a negative direction. Don't let him succeed! He knows your words aren't meaningless or powerless. They have creative power, just as God demonstrated when He created the heavens and the earth with His words. Now, we have the authority to do the same thing here on earth.

Contemplate the fact that your words hold incredible power. You have the power to influence and change the lives of all you share your world with ... your family, your friends, your neighbors, and the stranger passing by. It is your choice to use words that inspire and build or destroy and tear down. Remember, once said, your words cannot be retracted.

Pay attention to your language. Choose to speak life!

Ponder:

Consider the power of each of your words to edify and lift or to crush and destroy. How can you make a more concerted effort to choose to speak life into others?

Scripture:

Ephesians 4:29

Do not let any unwholesome talk come out of your mouths, but only what is helpful for building others up according to their needs, that it may benefit those who listen.

Proverbs15:4

The soothing tongue is a tree of life, but a perverse tongue crushes the spirit.

Prayer:

Oh Lord, help me to be cognizant of each word that proceeds from my mouth. Teach me to speak life-giving truths into the hearts of others. I will choose to speak life-giving words every day.

Day 4
Self-Talk

*T*he loudest voice we hear is our own voice. There is a voice inside of us … our self-talk. So quiet, but so powerful. Self-talk is a real deal. Self-talk is something we do naturally throughout our waking hours. It is a form of neuro linguistic programming. Because of its repetitive nature, it has the potential to mold and sculpt our consciousness.

Our enemy is a destroyer. He likes to bring lies in from early childhood and then convince us that these false beliefs are really our truth. He loves to develop strongholds in our lives that are full of lies. The only thing true about us is what God, the Knitter, Knower, Designer, and Creator, says about us. Can we differentiate these two voices? One brings life and builds. The other brings death and condemnation, usually a slow, burdensome death.

We have discussed that our thoughts bubble out into our words. Then we hear our "self" speak about our "self." What we speak often becomes our reality. If we think/say that we are dumb, stupid, or fat, we likely live a life behaving exactly as we speak. What if we agreed with our Creator and called ourselves fearfully and wonderfully made? A masterpiece? A daughter of the King? Strong and powerful? Would we live differently? When we think differently, we live differently. Changing the way you think changes your perspective which changes what you say and how you act in the world.

Positive self-talk: People are becoming more aware that positive self-talk is a powerful tool for increasing your self-confidence and curbing negative emotions. It is a phenomenal strategy for change. Positive words are good for our health as they help boost our confidence, improve our mood, eliminate stress, and improve heart health and well-being. People who can master positive self-talk are thought to be more confident, motivated, and productive. God created us for life and life abundantly. Does your self-talk align with His plan and Words over you?

Negative self-talk: We are also becoming aware of the effects of our inner critic, our negative words to our self. Negative self-talk can influence your self-esteem, your outlook on life, your energy levels, your relationships, and even your health. By taking note of negative self-talk, we can begin the necessary process of interrupting this destructive habit. It's time to silence that negative voice in our head and speak life and truth into our lives.

Our self-talk matters. Pay attention. More often than not, it is so routine to speak negatively about yourself and to yourself that you are completely unaware that you are doing it. I wonder if, for the next twenty-four hours, you would take the time to pay attention to your thoughts and also take notice of how you speak about yourself? Make a commitment to eliminate negative self-talk. Then align your thoughts and words with His power-filled truths.

Ponder:

In what ways can you align your self-talk with what God says about you? Are you kind to yourself? Do you know and speak out your identity in Christ?

Scripture:

1 Peter 5:8

Be alert and of sober mind. Your enemy the devil prowls around like a roaring lion looking for someone to devour.

Deuteronomy 30:19

This day I call the heavens and the earth as witnesses against you that I have set before you life and death, blessings and curses. Now choose life, so that you and your children may live.

Prayer:

Lord, help me believe that I am who You say that I am. Help Your voice be the loudest voice in my life. Let me speak the words of Your heart into my heart. I will choose to speak life-giving words every day.

Day 5

Words to Live By

Since the enemy lies to us, we need to make a decision to speak power and truth back to him! We need to take action steps to turn the tide of negative words and thoughts. We need power-filled WORDS TO LIVE BY. And then we need to speak them over and over until they reach deep into our hearts and our thoughts.

The truest thing about you is always what God says about you … not what you think or feel and not what others say, think, or do. We can become so paralyzed by lies and false beliefs that we miss the sweet plan of the Lord by a thousand miles. Study His Word. Let your faith speak and then ask God to help you with any unbelief.

There are actions that we can take to quit the negative self-talk. Just like any toxic bad habit, we can decide to stop this behavior. Ask the Holy Spirit to help you. It may take time, perseverance, attention, and strength to quit negative self-talk completely. For many of us it has become so deeply ingrained, it is almost second nature. Once you are aware of your negative self-talk, understand that you will need to keep interrupting yourself and your thoughts to stop it altogether. Becoming aware of this behavior is the key to quitting.

When we take control of our thoughts and our words, we take back our life! I challenge you to create a list of daily affirmations to speak to yourSELF … words to live by. This exercise is an important step in taking control of our thoughts and subsequently our words. It is time to practice speaking power and truth back into our lives by writing daily affirmations.

First, start with any negative thoughts or self-talk that dominate or frequent your thinking. List any lies that you are believing. What negative truths weigh you down and hinder you from living your best life? If our thoughts, self-talk, or words do not align with God's truth, we need to identify them.

Secondly, find scriptures as antidotes for these negative thoughts or lies. These spiritual truths can free you from those lies and strongholds/patterns. Take your thoughts and words captive to His truths! Choose words in alignment with the Word of God.

Lastly, study these scriptures and craft positive statements agreeing with them that you can claim and speak back into your life. These are positive affirmations that line up with TRUTH. Make your list. What affirmations can you speak to bring God's glory and better results to your life?

Speaking these affirmations daily will help you begin to take control of your life by getting control of your tongue. Refuse to speak anything other than the Word of God about your life or situation. Take authority over your life with scriptures and the power of your own spoken words of affirmation. These are your WORDS TO LIVE BY.

Ponder:

What are some thoughts and lies going through your head that do not align with God's Word? Ponder choosing life-giving truths to replace those thoughts. Speak them out to yourself daily.

Scripture:

Psalm 19:14

May these words of my mouth and this meditation of my heart be pleasing in Your sight, Lord, my Rock and my Redeemer.

Psalm 119:171-172

May my lips overflow with praise, for You teach me Your decrees. May my tongue sing of Your word, for all Your commands are righteous.

Prayer:

Lord, I want to speak and live from Your truths about me. Often, I feel so trapped in negativity and the weight of the world on my shoulders. Help me search for Your life-giving truths and meditate on them daily. I will choose to speak life-giving words every day.

Day 6

Social Media

I couldn't close this "Speaking" Bible plan about our words without commenting on the social media world that we live in. Without a doubt, social media is a HUGE influence on our thoughts and, therefore, on our minds. This is a very dominating source of input. Have you considered the positive, life-giving value of social media versus the negative and destructive trap that it usually is?

So many people these days suffer from anxiety and depression. I believe it could be traced back to an overwhelming amount of negative input as well as to a minimal amount of life-giving time in nature or the Word of God. Whether it is your TV, Facebook, Twitter, or Instagram, we all need to consider our screen time. Most of us would be surprised to learn the number of hours that we truly spend with our faces looking into a screen. Don't get me wrong. I do believe that there are some life-giving pictures, posts, and videos available. We need to recognize the distinctive value of what we put in our minds. There is so much on social media that is filling our minds with a lot of trash, self-glorification, and pontification through an excess of negative input. Most of us are ignorant to the correlation of screen time and depression. Most of us don't consider that INPUT affects OUTPUT to the degree that it does.

This world, the news, and our circumstances could have us feeling like we are walking in a desert or a dry wasteland. Our souls thirst for life and must be fed with life-giving food. His Words. His creation. His fellowship. Are you feeling depressed from walking too long in the desert or dry wasteland of social media and screen time? Come to the living water and let Him satisfy your soul. Choose your input. Consider turning off those screens and opening the Word of God. Ask Him to meet you there and make His Word alive. Then get outside. Take a walk. Fly a kite. Read a good book. Meet with a life-giving friend.

May I challenge you to take a sabbatical from social media? Pray about when to do this and then set an amount of time. It will be a fasting of sorts. Afterwards, if you feel that the sabbatical was valuable, make a commitment to limit your return to social media. Consider only posting uplifting or Christ-centered content. Since there has been so much division in our country, decide that you will bring something that would edify, inspire and speak life to a hurting world.

Life can be so much simpler and less stressful. We can have so much more hope. We need to use the time that we would be on a screen reading about stuff that doesn't matter and use it to spend time with Someone who does matter! It is not just screen time at fault, but the choice of input. Be wise.

If you want to live life, speak life, and give life to the fullest, then you must consider the INPUT of your days. Change your input, change your output. Our days are fleeting. Start NOW.

Ponder:

How can you make changes to decrease or eliminate your social media screen time? Consider only life-giving screen time when you choose to get on a screen. What are some productive things that you could do with your extra time?

Scripture:

Matthew 6:33

But seek first His kingdom and His righteousness, and all these things will be given to you as well.

Ephesians 5:16

Making the most of every opportunity, because the days are evil.

Prayer:

Oh Lord! Help me limit my screen time and increase my time with You. I want to live bold and speak life into the hearts of others. I know that it starts with me. I will choose to speak life-giving words every day.

CHAPTER 11

Searching for Wisdom

*D*o you ever find yourself scared of hard decisions? Do you ever feel unqualified to lead your kids or speak truth into your friends? Do you ever doubt your discernment and judgement? If so, there's good news: wisdom is yours if you will receive her.

Here are two truths you need to understand: 1) we all have something inside us that thinks there is something more to life and 2) we can't redo today as life is not a dress rehearsal. Knowing those truths, I thought it was high time I yielded to the fact that God says in James 1:5, "ask for wisdom and it shall be given to you," so that I'd actually have a clue how to live this life.

There's good news: wisdom is yours if you will receive her.

Day 1

Wisdom Calls

*P*roverbs 1:20 tells us, "Out in the open wisdom calls aloud, she raises her voice in the public square." If wisdom is calling and if life is fleeting, then are we listening? Let us incline our ears to the call of wisdom. In order to really listen well, I simply must choose to slow down and quiet my spirit. I need to ask for the very wisdom that is beckoning me. Our seeking is a response to God's grace, so we can seek His wisdom with hope. After all, He is the Creator and the Knower. We simply do not know and cannot know how to live "above and beyond all we could hope or imagine" or the "abundant life" without the help and the guiding wisdom of the Holy Spirit.

There is a mountain of knowledge beyond our awareness. It is impossible for us to know all that we do not know. So how then shall we live? The concept of MORE is buried in our souls. It is an internal longing for greater understanding and fruitfulness. Even the very magnitude of nature beckons us into this knowing. Ecclesiastes 3:11 states, "He has made everything beautiful in its time. He has also set eternity in the human heart; yet no one can fathom what God has done from beginning to end." Is the Lord beckoning us to the greater call of wisdom?

Knowing Jesus is our link into the call of wisdom. It all starts with Him. All other wisdom flows from our relationship with our living Lord. The wisest decision you can make to heeds wisdom's call is to begin a relationship with Jesus Christ, the wisdom of God. First Corinthians 2:16 tells us we have the mind of Christ, so if you call on Jesus, He will give you His wisdom for your situation.

Wisdom's call offers good judgement when we have none. It offers knowledge and discernment when needed. Wisdom also offers good advice, success, insight, and strength. Hungering for wisdom through a humble heart may be the wisest thing we ever do. So, stop now, bow your head and your will, and ask for more of His wisdom in your story, in your day, and in your choices.

Scripture is full of the treasures of wisdom. It says that whoever finds wisdom finds life and wins approval from the Lord. Wisdom leads us to life's answers. Time in the Word, searching the truths of wisdom, will be our greatest guiding light as the fear of the Lord is the beginning of wisdom. He is the great Knower and the great Redeemer of all that has been lost. He restores, renews, and refreshes at the fountain of wisdom. Let us drink from this fountain of living water, today and every day! Since wisdom calls out, let us be sure to answer.

Ponder:

How can I be more aware of the beckoning voice of wisdom calling out to me? In what ways can I prioritize the important pursuit of seeking daily wisdom for my life?

Scriptures:

Ecclesiastes 3:11

He has made everything beautiful in its time. He has also set eternity in the human heart; yet no one can fathom what God has done from beginning to end.

Proverbs 1:20-21

Out in the open wisdom calls aloud, she raises her voice in the public square; on top of the wall she cries out, at the city gate she makes her speech.

Prayer:

Lord, I want and need Your wisdom. Since You set eternity in my heart, teach me to live in Your eternal wisdom all the days of my life. I want to live from Your wisdom every single day.

Day 2

Practically Seeking Wisdom

Who doesn't want to be wise, given a choice? So how do you gain a heart of true wisdom? I was encouraged to meet a man years ago that was reputed to be a man of wisdom. I had never heard anyone introduced that way. Except for Solomon. I wanted that reputation. But how would I get from where I was to the reputation of a wise woman? I set out to ask the wisest friend I knew at the time. Then I have purposed to ask others. Here are some things I have learned.

True wisdom starts with the fear and reverence of the Lord, your Creator. Since He foreknew you and knit you on purpose and with purpose, seeking His heart for your life would be the wisest thing to do. No one is born wise; we must acquire wisdom from God if we are to be truly wise: Here are some other thoughts and practical ideas for gaining wisdom:

1. Study the Word. Read wise things. Since King Solomon's greatest desire was to have God's wisdom in order to lead His people (see 1 Kings 3 and 2 Chronicles 1), we can start with a study of Solomon's writing. Both the book of Proverbs and Ecclesiastes are stockpiles of wisdom. The primary way we gain godly wisdom is by learning God's Word (Psalm 119:169).

2. Seek humility because therein lies the truth. True humility requires honesty. We are not in charge tomorrow and cannot even manufacture our next breath let alone our next heartbeat. Seeking truth through humility will lead to a more fulfilling life of understanding of how we were created to love and serve others. Truly wise people are humble people as you can't be wise without being humble first.

3. Hang around and listen to wise people. Be a student of wise counselors that bear the fruit of wisdom in their own personal lives. "Plans fail for lack of counsel, but with many advisers they succeed"

(Proverbs 15:22). Nothing keeps us from good counsel more than our own pride. "Whoever walks with the wise becomes wise, but the companion of fools will suffer harm" (Proverbs 13:20). Those who want godly wisdom will choose their friends and heroes to be those who exhibit wisdom in their own personal lives.

4. Start each day from a yielded place of "not mine, but Thine" today Lord. Bow down daily so to speak. Live a life dead to your own plans and alive to the plans and the purposes of the Father. Be open to His Divine interruptions. Humbly step into the Greater Story. Let Him live through you as an instrument of peace and love into your world.

Godly wisdom can be attained and will not be hidden from us if we diligently seek it, ask for it, and fear God with our whole hearts.

Ponder:

What are some ways that you have chosen to practically be seeking wisdom? How can you increase your circle of wise counselors?

Scriptures:

Proverbs 9:10

The fear of the LORD is the beginning of wisdom, and knowledge of the Holy One is understanding.

Proverbs 11:2

When pride comes, then comes disgrace, but with humility comes wisdom.

Prayer:

Lord, help me to seek the depths of wisdom buried in the counsel of Your word. I desire to live a life reading wise things, listening to wise people, and making wise choices. I need your indwelling Holy Spirit to do such. I want to live from Your wisdom every single day.

Day 3

Worldy Wisdom – Godly Wisdom

*T*here's a difference between worldly wisdom and godly wisdom. Jesus highlighted these differences in His Sermon on the Mount (Matt. 5-7). For example, He said, "You have heard that it was said, 'Love your neighbor and hate your enemy.' But I tell you, love your enemies and pray for those who persecute you, that you may be children of your Father in heaven." Godly wisdom often is opposite our natural inclinations. Godly wisdom goes against the "conventional wisdom" of the day. It is not focused internally on self-preservation, but it is focused on furthering the kingdom of God.

Godly wisdom is, of course, from God and honors God. It is a wisdom that starts with the fear of the Lord and results in a holy life. Worldly wisdom, on the other hand, is not concerned with honoring God but with pleasing oneself. With worldly wisdom, we may become educated, street-smart, and have "common sense" that enables us to play the world's game successfully. Godly wisdom considers a completely different standard. With godly wisdom, we trade earthly values for biblical values (1 John 2:15–16). We recognize we are citizens of another kingdom, and we make choices that reflect that allegiance (Philippians 1:27; 3:20). Having godly wisdom means we strive to see life from God's perspective and live and behave accordingly.

Godly wisdom seems like foolishness to the world, when in reality, the wisdom of man is foolishness to God. The apostle Paul put it perfectly, writing that "the foolishness of God is wiser than men, and the weakness of God is stronger than men" (1 Cor. 1:25), so "Blessed is the one who finds wisdom, and the one who gets understanding, for the gain from her is better than gain from silver and her profit better than gold" (Prov. 3:13-14).

The fear of the Lord is the starting point in finding godly wisdom. For the Christ follower, it isn't a fear of being struck dead or the fear of hell, but a reverential holy fear that shows respect, and a high regard for God and His Word. Where there is a deep reverence for God and His Word, you'll find godly wisdom. We need to seek and ask for this godly wisdom as James tells us: "If any of you lacks wisdom, let him ask God, who gives generously to all without reproach, and it will be given him" (James 1:5).

We will spend our lives seeking and growing in godly wisdom. It is not a "one and done proposition." The Bible teaches us that age brings wisdom, as age brings more experiences and experiences give us greater wisdom. "Wisdom is with the aged and understanding in length of days. With God are wisdom and might; He has counsel and understanding" (Job 12:12-13 ESV). I invite you to spend your days pursuing godly wisdom and not simply the wisdom offered in this world.

Ponder:

How could you spend more of your time seeking godly wisdom versus just the wisdom and knowledge offered by our world? Do you recognize the difference between the eternal pursuit and the worldly pursuit?

Scriptures:

James 1:5

If any of you lacks wisdom, you should ask God, who gives generously to all without finding fault, and it will be given to you.

Proverbs 1:7

The fear of the Lord is the beginning of knowledge, but fools despise wisdom and instruction.

Prayer:

Oh Lord, I cast down my pride for worldly wisdom and ask that You beckon me to seeking the wisdom of Your ways and Your purposes. Open my eyes to the difference and the wasted time in pursuit of lesser values. I want to live from Your wisdom every single day.

Day 4

Proverbial Wisdom

*T*he book of Proverbs is filled with practical advice and life-principles that show us how to live wisely in the fear of God. It is a storehouse filled with verses about wisdom and folly. Below you will find helpful scripture. May these Bible verses about wisdom remind you of the truth of God as the source of all wisdom.

Proverbs 1:7

The fear of the LORD is the beginning of knowledge, but fools despise wisdom and instruction.

Proverbs 2:6

For the LORD gives wisdom; from his mouth come knowledge and understanding.

Proverbs 3:7

Do not be wise in your own eyes; fear the LORD and shun evil.

Proverbs 3:13

Blessed are those who find wisdom, those who gain understanding.

Proverbs 4:6-7

Do not forsake wisdom, and she will protect you; love her, and she will watch over you. The beginning of wisdom is this: Get wisdom. Though it cost all you have, get understanding.

Proverbs 9:10

The fear of the LORD is the beginning of wisdom, and knowledge of the Holy One is understanding.

Proverbs 10:8

The wise in heart accept commands, but a chattering fool comes to ruin.

Proverbs 10:23

A fool finds pleasure in wicked schemes, but a person of understanding delights in wisdom.

Proverbs 11:2

When pride comes, then comes disgrace, but with humility comes wisdom.

Proverbs 12:15

The way of fools seems right to them, but the wise listen to advice.

Proverbs 13:10

Where there is strife, there is pride, but wisdom is found in those who take advice.

Proverbs 13:1

A wise son heeds his father's instruction, but a mocker does not respond to rebukes.

Proverbs 13:20

Walk with the wise and become wise, for a companion of fools suffers harm.

Proverbs 14:1

The wise woman builds her house, but with her own hands the foolish one tears hers down.

Proverbs 15:12

Mockers resent correction, so they avoid the wise.

Proverbs 16:16

How much better to get wisdom than gold, to get insight rather than silver!

Proverbs 17:28

Even fools are thought wise if they keep silent, and discerning if they hold their tongues.

Proverbs 18:15

The heart of the discerning acquires knowledge, for the ears of the wise seek it out.

Proverbs 19:8

The one who gets wisdom loves life; the one who cherishes understanding will soon prosper.

Proverbs 19:20

Listen to advice and accept discipline, and at the end you will be counted among the wise.

Proverbs 29:11

Fools give full vent to their rage, but the wise bring calm in the end.

Ponder:

How much time do you invest in seeking wisdom from the Word? How might you prioritize a study of biblical wisdom?

Scriptures:

Psalm 32:8

I will instruct you and teach you in the way you should go; I will counsel you with My loving eye on you.

Psalm 119:105

Your word is a lamp for my feet, a light on my path.

Prayer:

Lord, I want to live from Your wisdom and not the foolish ways of the world. Help me seek You and the wisdom gained through the study of Your Word. I want to live from Your wisdom every single day.

Day 5

Characteristics of Godly Wisdom

What does godly wisdom look like? Could you recognize a truly wise person? Godly wisdom is found in and begins with our relationship with God. We find true wisdom by humbly submitting to Him and obeying His commands.

People characterizing wisdom have traded in some personal ego and self-interest for a good dose of humility and wisdom. They are standouts in this world as they are led by an eternal "others-oriented" agenda versus a self-centered success agenda. Whether watching our country's leaders or seeking to live our own lives with God's wisdom, it's important to know what His wisdom looks like so we can recognize it and live by it.

Remember that wisdom is not the same as knowledge. We can know a lot of stuff and still be very foolish. You don't have to look far to see examples. Here is a description of godly wisdom from Wayne Grudem in his book *Systematic Theology*.

"God's wisdom means that God always chooses the best goals and the best means to those goals. This definition goes beyond the idea of God knowing all things and specifies that God's decisions about what He will do are always wise decisions: that is, they always will bring about the best results (from God's ultimate perspective), and they will bring about those results through the best possible means."

If we applied this to us, if we want to be truly wise, we will make decisions and act in ways to move toward God's ultimate best for ourselves and for others.

The book of Proverbs discusses a long list of godly characteristics. But there's this great passage in James that highlights what godly wisdom looks like in just a few verses. The following characteristics are based on James 3:13-18.

- **Humble** – Wise people don't constantly brag, boast, or display a prideful attitude.

- **Pure** – Wise people have no malicious intentions. They are not filled with sin.

- **Good fruit** – Wise people live an upright, moral, and productive life.

- **Gentle** – Wise people treat others with kindness, care, and respect.

- **Considerate** – Wise people put the needs of others ahead of themselves whenever possible.

- **Peace-loving** – Wise people don't foster division and tension. Instead, they work to end strife and turmoil in a peaceful loving manner.

- **Merciful** – Wise people demonstrate compassion, grace, and forgiveness to others.

- **Sincere** – Wise people are genuine, real, and honest; not deceitful, hypocritical, or false.

- **Impartial** – Wise people are fair and just. They do not show partiality to others for their own benefit.

Do you know anyone who is wise? Do they reflect the character qualities listed above? Based on this list, do you consider yourself to be wise? This list might challenge each of us. I want my life to be a display of godly wisdom. What about you?

Ponder:

In what ways does my life reflect godly wisdom? Which of the above character traits do I need to develop and work on?

Scriptures:

Proverbs 8:17

I love those who love Me, and those who seek Me find Me.

James 3:17

But the wisdom that comes from heaven is first of all pure; then peace-loving, considerate, submissive, full of mercy and good fruit, impartial and sincere.

Prayer:

Lord, I want to be a reflection of your character to a hurting world. I need Your Holy Spirit to live through me to produce these qualities so that I can serve You and others in a greater capacity. I want to live from Your wisdom every single day.

CHAPTER 12

How Shall We Pray?

Over the years, many women have told me, "I want to pray. I mean, *really* pray and encounter Jesus like I hear about—but how?" Good question. Many of us approach prayer as a routine or a tradition. It's something we're supposed to do, but not something we really *get*. We want to, but how? Where is the power we long to experience? How are we to pray to God?

I remember standing on a mountaintop in California, wondering at His creation and being re-awakened to the truth of what it means to pursue a close relationship with God the Father. He isn't distant. He's a loving Abba Father who is intimately waiting for a conversation with me. He wants to communicate with me through prayer. He is my Father! He is our Father! When asked by His disciples, Jesus modeled the perfect prayer for us in Matthew 6; one that starts by soaking in God's holiness and then illustrates options in prayer so that we may live to honor His name.

Day 1

Our Example

*P*rayer affects all things. Nothing is more conspicuous in the life of Jesus Christ than prayer. He prayed often. Jesus prayed because He could do nothing without God, and neither can we. He knew His purpose was to reflect the heart of the Father.

God blesses the person who prays. Prayer is like going out on a long voyage into the heart of God. It enriches us, and it enriches the lives of those we are praying for. Our personal prayer life is critically important to building our relationship with God. Prayer is a conversation communicating my heart to my heavenly Father. For me, intimacy with God is the pinnacle of rich and successful living. The more communication … the more communion. The more communion … the more confidence. The more confidence … the more trust. The more trust … the more rest. I choose to live a life of quiet assurance and confident trust. It starts with prayer and a vibrant relationship of communion with my Savior.

Jesus' entire life was lived in close communication with His Father. What a great example for us! He often "went to the mountain to pray." At a minimum, His example teaches us to get away from the other voices and noises in our lives. The Word tells us to pray without ceasing, but, at least periodically, we need to silence the surrounding noise to hear the voice of the ONE. Jesus prayed anywhere and everywhere. He prayed in the Temple, in the Garden, in the wilderness, and on the Cross. He prayed with others but, more importantly, He prayed alone.

Take time right now to stop and pray. Ask God to help you develop a consistent life of prayer. I am convinced that your prayers matter. Prayers are powerful and effective when prayed for from a heart seeking the Lord's best. He says that if we ask not, we get not. Ask in accordance with His greater will for your life. Then trust.

I wonder if our Father's heart does a happy dance when we go to Him in prayer like I do when my children call me on the phone to connect and communicate. I bet He does. And I bet He is waiting for you right now. Go ahead. Reach out to Him in prayer today.

Start a new daily habit of prayer. When asked, Jesus directly taught His disciples how to pray. Let's learn from His example.

Ponder:

How much time do you spend in communication and in communion with your Creator, Knitter, and Knower? Consider reprioritizing prayer as a top priority. Jesus did.

Scriptures:

Luke 5:16

But Jesus often withdrew to lonely places and prayed.

Luke 6:12

One of those days Jesus went out to a mountainside to pray and spent the night praying to God.

Prayer:

Lord, I want to be in an intimate relationship with You, but I seem to continue to get side-tracked daily. Help me follow the example of Jesus and prioritize time in prayer with You. I will pray every day to develop a closer relationship with You.

Day 2

The Foundation

What is the foundation for our prayers? Our impetus for prayer should be our ongoing relationship with God, who is our Father, Creator, and Sustainer. He beckons us into relationship with Him. A personal prayer life is critical in building a close relationship with God.

The disciples witnessed that prayer was a significant foundational part of Jesus' life. In Luke 11, they came to Jesus and said, "Lord, teach us to pray." Jesus then used The Lord's Prayer as a model. Let us learn from His Word together.

1) **"This, then, is how you should pray: Our Father…"**

   First things first! Acknowledge that our prayers are to God THE Father and to God OUR Father. He is THE Father of all that has been created and yet He is OUR Father. Jesus is making it clear here that we are part of His family, and, as children, we can come to our loving Father like a good and loving Dad.

2) **"… in heaven, hallowed be Your name."**

   We need to recognize that we are praying to the infinite and sovereign God of the Universe. This is not a casual position but one involving an internal bowing down of ourselves as we align with His holiness. We must enter prayer with an attitude acknowledging Him as being holy, consecrated, and worthy of praise, honor, and glory.

3) **"Your kingdom come, Your will be done, on earth as it is in heaven."**

   Don't know about you, but I have a personal nature, usually for self and for gain. We are all selfish. But God has a will that none should perish, but all would come unto repentance which leads to eternal life. Jesus exemplified the spirit of yielding to the Father, His Father, Our Father. He said "... Not my will but Thine be done." This is our example to pray for, and in accordance with, His will being done on this earth as it is in heaven. His will for our living the kingdom of heaven on this earth is clearly spelled out in our "owner's manual," His Word.

The foundation for our prayer is that we are praying to our Holy Father, God, and Creator. He has designed us for His purposes here on earth. When you pray, do you pray to YOUR personal heavenly Father who is good and holy? Do you pray for His will, His way? Or your will, your way?

Ponder:

Do you recognize that you have a loving heavenly Father in which to pray? He is holy and He loves you and wants a relationship with you. He wants you to live in the peace of heaven while on earth.

Scriptures:

Luke 11:1

One day Jesus was praying in a certain place. When He finished, one of His disciples said to Him, "Lord, teach us to pray, just as John taught his disciples."

Matt 6:9-10

"This, then, is how you should pray: 'Our Father in heaven, hallowed be your name, your kingdom come, your will be done, on earth as it is in heaven ...'"

Prayer:

Lord, thank You that You are MY personal Abba Father. Teach me that the foundation of my prayer is who You are and not what I want. You alone are worthy. I will pray every day to develop a closer relationship with You.

Day 3

Petition and Forgiveness

*I*n Luke 11, Jesus also teaches about petition and forgiveness in the Lord's Prayer. So far, in Jesus' teaching example, we have been taught the foundation of our prayers: His position, His holiness, and His will, His way. Now we move on to the prayer of petition and forgiveness.

4) "Give us this day our daily bread." (petition)

Jesus' words here were intentional. Each word is important. He GIVES to US all that we need for DAILY provision. Period! The Greek word for "give" is also translated "to supply or furnish necessary things." Bread was a powerful symbol of God's provision for His people in the Old Testament. This petition teaches us to come to God in a spirit of humble daily dependence, asking Him to provide what we need to sustain us from day to day. We are not given license to ask for great riches, but we are encouraged to make our needs known to Him, trusting that He will provide. It is more about an attitude of communion and life together than about demands for food. This causes me to evaluate my choice of daily dependence versus my rogue independence and ideas on sustenance and provision. We actually need very little for sustenance. Jesus did not model praying for frills, wants, or objects of desire. Daily provision is a thought.

5) "And forgive us our debts, as we also have forgiven our debtors." (forgiveness)

Forgiveness is imperative for effective prayer and successful living. Not only are we to pray with a recognition of our sin nature within but with a humility that reaches out to forgive others with the same. We all suffer from an inherited sin condition. No one is exempt. But, by the blood of Jesus, our new nature is redeemed. We get to receive this grace and we must offer this grace of forgiveness to others. We receive the forgiveness of our heavenly Father. We, then, become the vessel through which that same forgiveness can flow through us and out to others. In, through, and out ... just like that. Simple. We are His vessels of forgiveness to a hurting world.

Let us all learn the beauty of dependence for daily provision. Life would be so much simpler if we could walk in this manner of faith. Less messy. Less cluttered with wants and waste. Also let us learn the power and the privilege of receiving His forgiveness and then passing it on to all in our lives.

Ponder:

How can I choose to live with less *wants* and live with the simplicity of basic *needs* ... my daily bread? Since God has forgiven me of much, who can I extend forgiveness to?

Scriptures:

Matt 6:11-12

Give us today our daily bread. And forgive us our debts, as we also have forgiven our debtors.

Philippians 4:19

And my God will meet all your needs according to the riches of His glory in Christ Jesus.

Prayer:

Lord, help me empty my life of unnecessary things that weigh it down. Teach me to live within my needs versus drowning in my wants. I need only You. Forgive me for the times that I am not quick to forgive others as You teach. I will pray every day to develop a closer relationship with You.

Day 4

Guidance and Protection

When teaching the disciples. Jesus continued his teaching about guidance, temptation and protection.

6) "And lead us not into temptation ..." (guidance)

Let's get this clear: The Lord never leads us into temptation. James 1:13 says, "When tempted, no one should say, 'God is tempting me.' For God cannot be tempted by evil, nor does He tempt anyone." So, what does Jesus mean? The Scriptures tell us that we all face temptations. We know that trials and temptations will come. When we are in the vulnerable place of being tempted, we need God's indwelling power and strength to overcome the temptation. He will provide a way out.

We know that temptations come from Satan. We also see in James 1:14 that temptation can originate in us as well. We are often tempted when we are "carried away and enticed by our own lust". We allow ourselves to think certain unhealthy thoughts, allow ourselves to go places we should not go, and make poor decisions based on our lusts or sin nature that lead us into the temptation.

All our efforts to resist temptation will be weak and ineffective unless they are powered by the Holy Spirit. Colossians 3:2 says, "Set your mind on the things above, not on the things that are on earth." If our minds are filled with the latest TV shows, music, and all the rest the culture has to offer, we will be bombarded with tempting messages and images that inevitably lead to sinful lusts. But if our minds are filled with the majesty and holiness of God and the love of Jesus, we will find that our interest in the lusts of the world diminish and disappear. Without the Word's influence on our minds, we are open to anything Satan wants to throw at us.

7) "... but deliver us from the evil one." (protection)

As addressed, there is evil in this world, ultimately led by the devil himself. Praying for deliverance from the evil one is a clear admission of the battleground. We know who ultimately wins as "[...] greater is He that is in you than he that is in the world (or in our temptation)" (1 John 4:4 ESV). For believers, God lives IN us. He who is within you is greater. Greater than any problem. Greater than any difficulty. Greater than the devil. Greater than anything you will ever face. As we submit ourselves to the work of the Father and resist the devil, the enemy will flee, and we will be delivered. As we live yielded to Him, He is our ultimate protection.

Reflect on each component of the Lord's prayer. God calls us to pray to Him on a regular basis. This prayer is only one model, so it should not dissuade us from praying otherwise. The "Lord's Prayer" is a beautiful way to follow the example of Jesus' teaching and be gospel-centered during your time with God.

Ponder:

How have you been intentional in seeking the Lord's guidance and protection from evil. In what additional ways can you "set your mind on things above and not of this earth?"

Scriptures:

James 1:13-14

When tempted, no one should say, "God is tempting me." For God cannot be tempted by evil, nor does He tempt anyone; but each person is tempted when they are dragged away by their own evil desire and enticed.

1 Corinthians 10:13_

No temptation has overtaken you except what is common to mankind. And God is faithful; He will not let you be tempted beyond what you can bear. But when you are tempted, He will also provide a way out so that you can endure it.

Day 5

When and Where to Pray

*G*ood communication is one of the keys to any successful relation-ship. As relational beings made in the image of God, we all recognize this vital aspect of intimate close relationships. That is why it is helpful to remember that prayer is, as John Calvin often referred to it, "conversation with God."

When should we pray? Like conversation within a healthy marriage, prayer is ideally frequent and organic. If I only spoke to my spouse during scheduled periods of time either at the beginning or end of the day—or worse still, only on Sundays—there could be a problem. At the same time, scheduling purposeful moments to have deeper, uninterrupted conversation, is extremely healthy. Scripture charges us both to "pray without ceasing" in a very organic manner (1 Thess. 5:17) and also records Christians praying at set times and not just accidentally stumbling into it.

It didn't take me long as a Christian to learn that if I did not set aside a daily time to pray, the busyness of life would all too easily get in the way. To not prioritize prayer is to prioritize something else. At the same time, I also learned that when I emphasize a set time to pray, I have the tendency to begin treating it like just another item on my to-do list.

Our whole life should be filled with prayer. The ideal would be to walk in constant communion and fellowship with God. The preeminent way to stay close to the Lord and the best way to fight against sin is to fight on our knees.

WHEN should we pray?

- **All the time:** 1 Thessalonians 5:17, Luke 18:1, Ephesians 6:18

- **In the morning:** Psalm 5:3, Mark 1:35

- **In the afternoon:** Acts 3:1, Acts 10:30

- **In the evening:** Luke 1:10, Matthew 14:23

- **Three times a day:** Daniel 6:10, Psalm 55:16-17

- **Before meals:** 1 Corinthians 10: 30-31, Mark 8:6

- **Continually:** 1 Thessalonians 5:17

Pray when you are sad or when you are happy. Pray when you are mad or wallowing in self-pity. Pray when you are suffering, in trouble, or in distress. Pray when you feel alone. Pray when you need guidance/direction. Pray when you need to cry out in pain or in worship. Anytime. All the time.

WHERE should we pray?

I believe the answer to where we should pray is liberatingly simple: we should pray wherever we need to pray. Scripture does not restrict prayer only to within a church building. We should pray where we need to pray.

- **In private:** Matthew 6:6

- **In bed:** Psalm 63:6

- **At the river:** Acts 16:13

- **On the seashore:** Acts 21:5

- **At the well:** Genesis 24:12-13

- **In God's house:** Luke 2:36-37

- **On the battlefield:** Joshua 10:12-13

Pray in private, together, alone, in bed, at the river, on the mountain, in the wilderness, in nature, on the seashore, at the well, in God's house, in the garden, in the closet, and on the battlefield. Pray everywhere and anywhere!

Ponder:

How can you increase your intimacy with God by more communication through prayer? What priorities do you need to adjust to prioritize time in prayer?

Scriptures:

Phil. 4:6

Do not be anxious about anything, but in every situation, by prayer and petition, with thanksgiving, present your requests to God.

James 4:8a

Come near to God and He will come near to you.

Prayer:

Lord, I want to be close to You and to know Your ways but my life seems so hectic. Help me set aside time just for us. You and me. Communication and communion. I will pray every day to develop a closer relationship with You.

CHAPTER 13

Marriage Matters

*H*ow do we make it until "Death do us part!" with enduring, lasting, vibrant love and commitment?

After thirty-five years of marriage, having four kids in five years, and enduring hardships and teenage rebellion, I've earned a deep appreciation for the life-long love in marriage.

Not sure if you've run into this truth, but love takes work! The work of love starts with the words "I do" and ends with "till death do us part." It's what you do in between those phrases that matters. The work of love is an investment in your heart, your home, and your family. Roll up your sleeves, and let's get to work on a marriage that matters.

Day 1

A Cord of Three Strands

God is a multiplier. He multiplied the fish and the loaves to feed 5,000 hungry souls. These two miracles of Jesus, known as the feeding of the multitude, are recorded in the gospels. He can multiply our effectiveness, our love, and our wisdom. But He must be included and invited into the process. Marriages need God to multiply love.

Before I married my husband, we discussed the truth that if we love God FIRST, then we could love each other BETTER. We also discussed that without God's indwelling Spirit, we would be just left to love one another in our own effort, which could be sadly lacking at many times. Ecclesiastes 4:12 states, "Though one may be overpowered, two can defend themselves. A cord of three strands is not quickly broken." I wanted a strong marriage. We needed to be a cord of three strands.

The strand passage from Ecclesiastes illustrates that the union of two Christians bound together in Christ are stronger than the individuals themselves. We believe that Christian marriage is about more than the union of one man and one woman. The Bible teaches us that God performs a miracle in our marriage, uniting us together in a covenant relationship with Him as one. The Cord of Three Strands is a symbol of that sacred union created on your wedding day.

So, what is a strand? A strand is a part that combines with other parts to form a whole. In the example of a thread, the strand is made with each individual thread twisted around and entwined with each other. The purpose of "threading" is to provide simultaneous execution of parallel parts. When lives or tasks run in parallel, the process of threading makes a strand that is stronger than each individual part.

What are the three strands of marriage? A good marriage takes three: you, your soon-to-be spouse, and God. God is love and teaches us to love. By keeping Him at the center of your marriage, woven into and intertwined through every aspect of it, His love will continue to bind you together as one.

Joshua 24:15 states "…choose this day whom you will serve … but as for me and my household, we will serve the Lord." Bringing God into your marriage must be a deliberate choice. In a great marriage, God is intertwined in the relationship as the third and higher authority. He can multiply the results in your marriage as long as you have given the Holy Spirit total permission to live through each of you to love the other. This involves dying to yourself and fighting for the three-corded STRAND of your marriage.

Ponder:

In your marriage, how can you get better at yielding to your third and higher authority? Discuss the "threading of parallel parts" with your spouse as a plan to strengthen your marriage.

Scripture:

Ecclesiastes 4:9-12

Two are better than one, because they have a good return for their labor: If either of them falls down, one can help the other up. But pity anyone who falls and has no one to help them up. Also, if two lie down together, they will keep warm. But how can one keep warm alone? Though one may be overpowered, two can defend themselves. A cord of three strands is not quickly broken.

Matthew 18:20

For where two or three gathered in My name, there am I with them.

Prayer:

Oh Lord, Your ways are higher and greater than our ways. Draw us together in a place where Your love is the very core of our marriage. I will work on loving my spouse every single day as I know that my marriage matters.

Day 2

Focus on the Praiseworthy

*T*he day we get married, we are eager to say "YES" and "I DO" and "I WILL" till death do us part. Sure. Yes, and amen! Then what happens? What changes? When I told my father that I wanted to marry my hubby, I told him about all the great things that I loved about him. He was this, this, and this. And he could do that, that and even that. We were going to be different than all those married statistics of failure. We were going to soar through our marriage on our true love.

Several years later, after four children and two career adjustments, we were not soaring anymore. We were having to choose to love one day at a time. Drowning in a million things to do, I found myself resenting all the things that my husband "wasn't doing." So, who was in charge of the chaos in our lives? Who could I blame? I was overwhelmed by all my blessings, so to speak. I had a great husband and four growing children but found myself feeling discouraged and defeated.

At a business convention, we were challenged to make a list of ten things that we loved about our spouses and then place that list on our bathroom mirrors (to help us remember). And if we were feeling especially out of touch and could not think of ANYTHING that we loved about our spouse, we were challenged to ponder back to the engagement and pre-wedding period … and have that person write the list. You know, the person who was thrilled and willing to marry. In doing so, I was reminded about several reasons that I got married that just seemed to disappear in a fog of busyness. The enemy had come to destroy my marriage, but I was participating. I had been disobedient to God's Word that told me to focus on ALL THAT WAS PRAISEWORTHY about my husband, about my children, and about my full life.

Realizing that marriage was not a sprint but a marathon, I quickly decided that I was in charge of my mind and what I was dwelling on. No spouse or child is perfect, and we are all sinners. It takes a lot of love and grace to live with your tribe. But I was determined to start focusing on all that was praiseworthy and giving my control freak a rest. I was on a "praiseworthy hunt." After identifying anything that was edifying or uplifting about someone in our household, I would speak about it and celebrate it. Any act of kindness, generosity, and service became a party to celebrate. I want to challenge married couples to find that which is praiseworthy about your spouse and then celebrate in gratitude for such. You don't get it all. What a great treasure hunt to occupy your married days … searching for that which is praiseworthy!

Ponder:

How can you choose to focus more on the praiseworthy in your household and especially with your spouse? What are some concrete ideas to help you do so?

Scripture:

Philippians 4:8

Finally, brothers and sisters, whatever is true, whatever is noble, whatever is right, whatever is pure, whatever is lovely, whatever is admirable—if anything is excellent or praiseworthy—think about such things.

1 Thessalonians 5:16-18

Rejoice always, pray continually, give thanks in all circumstances; for this is God's will for you in Christ Jesus.

Prayer:

Lord, I want to obey Your Word to "focus on all that is praiseworthy," but I need Your help as I am often drowning in busyness or negative things. I ask You to blind me to the negative/death and open my eyes to the positive/life in my spouse. I will work on loving my spouse every single day as I know that my marriage matters.

Day 3
The Law of Entropy

*A*ll marriages take work! I graduated from college with a degree in petroleum engineering. In order to get an engineering degree, all engineers had to go through "core classes." One of these classes was called Thermodynamics. Crazy as it seems, I will be forever changed by learning and applying the "law of entropy" to my marriage. Simply stated, the law of entropy, the second law of thermodynamics, says that "in all energy exchange, if no energy enters or leaves the system, the potential energy of the state will be less than that of the initial state." Let me explain in English. The law of entropy tells us, by nature, disorder always increases. It tells us anything and everything that God or man has ever made will always move from order to disorder. Order is always followed by disorder without any outside input.

So now let's extrapolate that thought into our marriages. From the minute we say, "I do. Yes. Till death do us part," our marriages start heading towards "disorder." That could lead to hopelessness or to wisdom. Once we learn that our laws of nature cannot be changed, we can adapt to their truth. Such as, even if I don't BELIEVE in the law of gravity, whenever I let go of the apple in my hand it will still fall to the ground. The law is not dependent on my belief in it. The law of entropy simply told me, in layman's terms, that I had to work on my marriage or expect it to go south. Once I realized the absolute truth of this and compared it to the marriage statistics at hand, we decided to work on our marriage after we left the altar and walked down the aisle. Before our wedding day, we discussed the WORK of being married. We agreed to WORK on it while it was good so that we didn't have to WORK on it while it was bad. We all put in the WORK either way! This was an intentional choice for our marriage. It was an investment in our future happiness and the health of our future family.

Besides the daily choice to work on love, we added an annual retreat of sorts to make sure that our marriage was in a good place. After thirty-five years of marriage, I don't wonder why we have a healthy, loving marriage. We have been working on it for thirty-five years.

On our annual retreat here are a few thoughts/questions we consider:

1. What were the best and the worst events in our marriage that year?

2. What can I do to be a better spouse to you?

3. How can I show you more love?

4. What do I do that you love? Or dislike?

5. What are some new dreams/goals for us?

6. Etc...

Remember that your marriage takes the investment of work, work, and more work. If you are behind in this investment, be sure and start today.

Ponder:

How can you start or continue to work on your developing and deepening marriage love? What are some things you can do to make time to invest in this life-long commitment?

Scripture:

Colossians 3:23-24

Whatever you do, work at it with all your heart, as working for the Lord, not for human masters, since you know that you will receive an inheritance from the Lord as a reward. It is the Lord Christ you are serving.

Proverbs 14:23

All hard work brings a profit, but mere talk leads only to poverty.

Prayer:

Lord, I will never make it "until death do us part" without Your inspired help. Lead, direct, and guide us as we work to make honoring You the priority of our marriage. I will work on loving my spouse every single day as I know that my marriage matters.

Day 4

The Power of Forgiveness

*F*orgiveness brings personal freedom. Unforgiveness suffocates! Recently I asked my father-in-law the key to his seventy years of marriage. He said that the secret ingredient to seventy years of love was forgiveness. Since all of us are messy and will be on both sides of the forgiveness issue, we all need loads of grace and forgiveness. This is not a one-sided scenario.

All human beings are beautiful but messy ... #beautifulbutmessy. Each of us are beautiful because God doesn't make junk. Actually, He calls you His masterpiece. The first phrase of Ephesians 2:10 reads, "For we are God's masterpiece" (NLT). Other translations say that we are God's "accomplishment" (CEB), "workmanship" (ESV, KJV), or "God's handiwork" (NIV). In addition, you were fearfully and wonderfully made ... beautiful. You were knit and known by a good, good Father Creator. You were assigned purpose in your days. However, all of us beautiful individuals are also *messy* because of inherited sin. We are all sinners. It would not be right for us to "throw stones" at one another. That would be like a sinner calling a sinner *a sinner*. We all live in this human condition/dilemma together ... beautiful but messy.

Our souls were not designed for the anger, bitterness, depression, and malice that comes from unforgiveness. It is so unhealthy and unsatisfying. However, we all married imperfect human beings. This is the dilemma.

We don't always forgive others because they deserve it, but we forgive others because we deserve the peace of mind that it affords. Decide ahead of time that you will forgive others so that it will be your natural reaction, rather than resentment. Unforgiveness is like drinking a bitter poison but expecting the other person to die. We think that holding grudges of unforgiveness harms the other, but we are actually just harming ourselves.

The willingness to forgive is not just a sign of great maturity but also of great wisdom.

Knowledge is knowing we should forgive, but wisdom is actually doing it. Unforgiveness also messes with your health, not just your peace of mind.

Here are a few reasons to forgive:

- To free us from anger and bitterness

- To allow us to live in our divine design

- To free up space for our health and peace

- To release us from the torment of the issue

- To free us to be effective in the present

- To ensure that God will hear and answer our prayers

Forgiveness is not ignoring or disregarding a wrong done. It is not based on feelings but based on a choice. The TRUTH is that Christ is the source of all forgiveness! We will all struggle with forgiving others, forgiving ourselves, and battling offense if we don't find peace over just how forgiven we are in Christ. It is a FINISHED WORK. Walk in that truth!

We have His forever forgiveness! Let His forgiveness flow into you and then out to others through you!

Ponder:

Have you considered the idea of forgiving someone even before they hurt you because you know the value of that choice? What are areas of unforgiveness where you need to let God bring you into peace and healing?

Scripture:

Colossians 3:13

Bear with each other and forgive one another if any of you has a grievance against someone. Forgive as the Lord forgave you.

Ephesians 4:31-32

Get rid of all bitterness, rage and anger, brawling and slander, along with every form of malice.

Be kind and compassionate to one another, forgiving each other, just as in Christ God forgave you.

Prayer:

Lord, You have forgiven me of much. Help me to let go of past grievances and choose to extend forgiveness and receive new peace of mind. I need Your strength and power through me. I will work on loving my spouse every single day as I know that my marriage matters.

Day 5

Teammates for Life

When we marry, we become teammates for life. That sounds so simple. Then why do so many marriages end in divorce? There are marriage myths that most don't realize come with being a teammate.

One of the first myths of marriage is we all go into marriage expecting the exact same things from marriage. As lifelong teammates, the goal of loving "until death do you part" might be the common vision and plan, but the day-to-day strategies to get to that vision might vary widely. We all enter marriage with unspoken rules, varying shades of expectations, and unconscious role fulfillment that we bring from our past experiences or our perceptions.

Teammates for life must talk to get on the same page for conflict resolution. This important communication can happen either before or after an identified conflict. We each bring our past cultures and experiences into our marriages. New marriage partners/teammates would want to blend the BEST of both to come up with their own new culture and vision. Two are better than one as they have twice the experience and wisdom. It is not "his way" or "her way" but the new *"our way."*

Another marriage myth that undermines teammates is the thought that once they marry, everything will get better. Actually, merging two individuals into a common household brings many challenges. Every marriage is filled with trade-offs. The most difficult trade-off is the loss of the ideal image of your partner. We cannot know everything about our spouse before we marry them. Love will be difficult on its way to becoming deep and lasting.

It is also a myth of marriage that everything that is bad will disappear with marriage. Getting married does not fix our personal past pains. Ignoring them doesn't fix them either. Marriage is not a cure-all for problems, but with time, it can become an agent for greater healing. The myth that your spouse will make you whole is a lie. Marriage is a

God-given way to improve, sharpen, and challenge each other to new heights of personal living. However, neither marriage nor your partner can make you whole. This is individual work. Your team and marriage relationship can only be as healthy as each individual teammate. That is why exploring your personal well-being as an individual as well as a teammate is vital for enduring a life-long love as marriage partners.

Being on the same team doesn't mean that we can't fight, but the real fight is with our enemy that seeks to destroy our marriages and all that is good. When we come into agreement that there will always be a destructive force contending for our marriages and our homes, as teammates we can then identify the real enemy and know where the real battle is. This daily battle starts on our knees … teammates together.

Ponder:

What are some ways I can be a better teammate? How can I seek a greater personal wholeness so that I can contribute to my marriage from that wholeness and strength?

Scripture:

Romans 15:5-6

May the God who gives endurance and encouragement give you the same attitude of mind toward each other that Christ Jesus had, so that with one mind and one voice you may glorify the God and Father of our Lord Jesus Christ.

Proverbs 27:17

As iron sharpens iron, so one person sharpens another.

Prayer:

Lord, help me find my wholeness in You alone so that I can be a better teammate to my spouse. I need all of You in all of me to do so. I will work on loving my spouse every single day as I know that my marriage matters.

Day 6

Soul Mates

*B*ecoming soul mates is one of your marriage's highest priorities. Finding soul satisfaction in the one you marry is a life-long, beautiful, and worthy pursuit. Instead of saying, "I married my soul-mate," let's challenge ourselves to the thought of "becoming soulmates" with the one that we married. Tending our own souls and the soul of our marriage is like tending a garden. It takes regular care and cannot be ignored for undue periods of time. So how do we go about doing that? It won't happen accidentally. Let's ponder things that tie souls together.

As spiritual beings, one of our first priorities would be to find a common place/practice for worship and spiritual development. Come into agreement on a plan to gather with like-minded believers and hear truth from an inspired and outside source. This weekly practice will provide life-giving input and conversation that will increase soul ties.

Serving others together is another healthy part of a soul-satisfying marriage. There is something deeply rewarding about serving others. It is not only good for the ones you serve; it also makes us happier and healthier too. These good feelings are reflected in the biology of our souls. Serving alongside your spouse not only connects you to each other but also to others, creating stronger communities where you live. Scientists believe that altruistic behavior releases endorphins in the brain, producing the positive feeling known as the "helper's high." This doesn't just make the world better—it also makes you better. Studies indicate that the very act of giving back into others and our communities boosts our happiness, health, self-esteem, and sense of well-being. Feeling good about yourself is something no one can take away from you. Serving others together is a fulfilling soul-tying marriage activity.

Another way to intentionally build your soul connection with your spouse is through shared activities. A marriage cannot thrive with two ships just passing in the night. We must actually enjoy times together outside the responsibilities of our home and our children. Consider a weekly or periodic date night. Take turns planning what that looks like. Also consider a physical activity together like walking, sports, working out together, etc. We all did activities together when we were dating. Keep that spark alive.

And finally, but maybe most importantly, consider praying together. This can become a habit that pays HUGE dividends. There is something particularly romantic when our loved one takes our concerns before the Lord. That is not the reason to pray together ... just a side benefit. You can simply start by praying at meals together, then move to praying over heavy heart concerns. The ultimate would be to end up praying daily together as a soul-tying habit for love and connection.

"Neglect the rest of the world if you have to but never neglect each other" (Ann Landers). Whatever you choose, be intentional. Recognizing the importance of soul-ties and the wise investment to develop such, is a key foundation for a good marriage.

Ponder:

What are some choices you can make to catalyze greater soul-connections with your spouse? How are you intentionally gardening the soul of your marriage?

Scripture:

Matthew 6:33

But seek first His kingdom and His righteousness, and all these things will be given to you as well.

Colossians 2:2

My goal is that they may be encouraged in heart and united in love, so that they may have the full riches of complete understanding, in order that they may know the mystery of God, namely, Christ.

Prayer:

Lord, I want a marriage that reflects and honors You and our covenant vow of love together. Guide us to connecting our souls to You first and then to one another as an outpouring of that relationship. I will work on loving my spouse every single day as I know that my marriage matters.

Day 7

Celebrate the Difference

While we were engaged, we had the privilege of having dinner with Florence Littauer, author of the book Personality Plus. She admonished us with a powerful truth that I will never forget. She said that Bryan and I had such different personalities that we were attracted to the varying strengths in each other. Then she said, "The difference in your personalities, that attracted you to marry each other, will become a bigger issue in the future. Either those differences will draw you closer together as a stronger 'whole,' or those differences will drive you apart. You will decide which is true!" What? It will be up to us whether the differences make us strong or separate us. Wow! Such a powerful thought to consider.

"He created them male and female and blessed them" (Gen. 5:2). This scripture doesn't say that He created them as simply "people" … but as male and female. Why did God create two sexes? Because they are different and need each other's differences! Besides the obvious anatomical differences, there are an array of compelling differences that strengthen the partnership of the marriage bond between a man and a woman. Understanding, celebrating, and even appreciating these differences can enhance our marriages. Man and woman are not created equal. They are both created uniquely, perfectly, and functionally different. Viva la difference!

Why are gender roles so important in marriage? For one, God designed marriage, and when people do not follow His design, the marriage is destined for design problems. It is important for us to know and follow His design, even when it is countercultural or contrary to what we are accustomed to. In the creation story, God first made Adam and then fashioned Eve as his helper. Genesis 2:18 says, "The Lord God said, 'It is not good for the man to be alone. I will make a helper suitable for him.'" Suitable for him! From the very beginning, we can see that God is a God of *order* even as indicated by the *order* of creation. His original intention was for the husband to lead the marriage, with the "suitable helper" in his wife.

There are always exceptions to the rule, but research points to a fundamental difference between the sexes: Men focus on achievement and women focus on relationships. This over-simplified glance compliments the thought that women, generally speaking, want love and men, generally speaking, want respect. As women need to be heard, known, cherished, and loved, men need to be admired and respected. Wise couples find ways to accommodate one another's needs regardless of their opinion of the validity of that need. Romans 12:10 suggests that we are to be devoted to and delight in honoring one another. This is a choice as well as a powerful concept!

None of us function or thrive in the "cage of expectations." That is one sure way to clearly destroy the joy of marriage. However, we all share one thing in common. Husbands and wives both depend on communication to keep their relationship healthy. It is the lifeblood of every successful marriage. Couples who can't communicate well, by speaking clearly and listening carefully, soon fall apart. It is a major key to bridging the gender gap. Carefully listening to your partner not only shines a light on gender differences but is the quickest path to engender more intimacy. Communicate and then give each other the grace to grow.

The gender differences, if heeded and accounted for, can become an area for developing greater understanding and intimacy in your marriage. However, ignoring gender differences will likely leave your marriage on the brink of disaster. You are not *competing* with your spouse, but you are *completing* the design and needs of your marriage.

Ponder:

How aware am I of gender differences in my marriage? What can I do to understand and celebrate our God-given design and differences?

Scripture:

Genesis 1:27

So God created mankind in His own image, in the image of God He created them; male and female He created them.

Genesis 2:18

The Lord God said, "It is not good for the man to be alone. I will make a helper suitable for him."

Prayer:

Lord, I recognize that You created males and females differently. Help me to wrap My arms around Your purposes and plans for such in my marriage. I will work on loving my spouse every single day as I know that my marriage matters.

Day 8

More Marriage Matters

*H*ere are some additional suggestions (in random order) to enhance your marriage experience:

- Catch your spouse in the act of doing something good or positive, then verbalize it.

- Love takes work. Ask your spouse if they would be willing to work towards a great marriage with you.

- Spend quality time with each other – while understanding that each spouse has other time commitments.

- Recognize each spouse needs some space for personal autonomy.

- Show interest in each other's opinions, ideas, work, and activities. There is so much you can learn from one another.

- Physical touches like hugging, holding hands, and other simple physical gestures are vital no matter what the couple's sexual life is like.

- Practice generosity of thought, spirit, and action towards each other.

- Acknowledge there are other important people in each spouse's life: friends, their family, colleagues, etc.

- Make time and create opportunities to have fun and laugh together often.

- Develop communication skills. Especially be a good listener.

- Dream together ... if not regularly ... at least quarterly.

- Be sure to set aside time weekly (date night) to prioritize time for you two. Your kids need to see this! Have some fun times planned.

- Daily plan a random act of kindness towards your spouse ... not meals or normal routine stuff. Something unusual.

- Keep a strong relationship with the Lord as oftentimes you will need God alone to love your spouse through you.

- Practice the habit of happiness ... would you like to be married to you?

- Seek wisdom about your marriage from above. Ask God to teach you how to love your spouse better. Study 1 Cor. 13.

- Work with your spouse to create a mission/vision statement for your marriage and family.

- Never put your spouse on a guilt trip or shame them with your tone of voice. If you slip into this, then quickly apologize as God never shames us!

- Ask your spouse what things you do that they love and what things you do that irritate them and then learn to be better ... not perfect ... but better.

- Study your spouse's love language (*The Five Love Languages* by Gary Chapman) and be sure to speak it to them. When in doubt, speak a bit of each love language regularly (touch, words, gifts, time, and service).

- Become a student of your spouse and get a PhD in them. Learn how to better understand and love them from their point-of-view.

- Take some form of personality test for greater understanding of one another.

- Consider taking a marriage-based "strengths assessment" to enhance marital understanding.

- Set personal boundaries around extramarital relationships.

- Say something nice, kind, or up-lifting to your spouse daily.

- Develop close, quality couple friendships that will uphold, encourage, and inspire your marriage.

- Develop life-giving girl/guy friends outside your marriage to help satisfy your relational needs.

Ponder:

Since marriages really do matter, name some ways that you can be more intentional about addressing additional "marriage matters" listed above. Highlight and initiate a plan to improve together.

Scripture:

1 Corinthians 13:4-7

Love is patient and kind; love does not envy or boast; it is not arrogant or rude. It does not insist on its own way; it is not irritable or resentful; it does not rejoice at wrongdoing but rejoices with the truth. Love bears all things, believes all things, hopes all things, endures all things.

Ephesians 5:33

However, let each one of you love his wife as himself, and let the wife see that she respects her husband.

Prayer:

Lord, we know that marriages matter. We also know that marriages are Your chosen way to build families. Help us to be cognizant of greater ways to love one another. I will work on loving my spouse every single day as I know that my marriage matters.

CHAPTER 14

Navigating Teenage Rebellion

*D*o you have teenage kids who make you want to scream at them, cry, and hold them tight in your arms with love all at once? I've been there! And any other mother who has raised a teen. Raising a teen is a wonderful gift, but it is not for the faint of heart. Join this chapter as we talk about how to love and pursue our children through the struggles of teenage rebellion.

Teen years are a crazy time full of hormones that cause a young adult to want to "rise up and have dominion over all of their earth." As you raise children to be all God calls them to be, the enemy can come into this tender changing teen season to divert and derail any progress.

As we navigate through these teenage years as mothers, we may often feel like we are in a confusing, dark season with only a tiny match to light our way. It's OK to feel under qualified, but important to remember that though you and your teen may get into some heated discussions at times, your child is NOT your enemy.

Day 1

Surprised by Rebellion?

*R*ebellion is within all of us, not just teenagers. No one is excluded. Rebellion is defined as "a person who rises against authority." Rebellion comes from sin, which is defined as "a transgression against divine law." Pride is defined as "a high or inordinate opinion of one's own importance." Rebellion, sin, and pride started in the Garden of Eden and have passed through the generations to all mankind. That includes you and me. It includes those we marry and those we birth. As Pastor John MacArthur states, "Sin is in our nature, it's in our disposition, it's in our humanness. It's not just in our physical body, it's in our minds, it's in our affections, it's in our feelings, it's in our emotions, it's in our will."

So why are we so surprised by rebellion in our teenagers? Hebrews 12:1 speaks of the "sin that so easily entangles us." When our sons and daughters go through adolescence, hormones hit hard. I believe hormones are just one way they try to "rise up and have dominion over *their* earth." This is a confusing time for them and can often be a confusing time for us as parents. There were times I thought, "I never taught you to speak that way (disrespectfully)," or "Where did my sweet little boy go?" This is a natural time of passage from being a young child into becoming a young adult. We must understand that the "becoming" process can surprise the best of us.

Hindsight showed me that the enemy was trying to rob, kill, and destroy the joy of those years. He confused my kids, which ultimately led to some rebellious behaviors. They were blinded and disoriented. We can all be blinded and disoriented at times. As parents, we need to remember that hormones and adolescence are a part of maturing and growing up. We need to help our teens navigate this transitional time with wisdom and grace. Children are a gift from God and can be some of life's greatest teachers—to the parent who is willing to learn. I hope to help you navigate these teenage years with sanity and grace.

Ponder:

Consider the rebellion in your own heart as you consider the rebellion in others. A sinner cannot throw a stone at another sinner. Rebellion is within all of us. Lord have mercy!

Scripture:

Genesis 3:6-7

When the woman saw that the fruit of the tree was good for food and pleasing to the eye, and also desirable for gaining wisdom, she took some and ate it. She also gave some to her husband, who was with her, and he ate it. Then the eyes of both of them were opened, and they realized they were naked; so they sewed fig leaves together and made coverings for themselves.

Romans 5:12

Therefore, just as sin entered the world through one man, and death through sin, and in this way death came to all people, because all sinned.

Prayer:

Lord, You are never surprised. Help me navigate the pride, rebellion, and sin in my life and in the lives of those that I love. I will love my teens even when I don't understand or are surprised by their choices.

Day 2

The Daily Battlefield

*D*aily, we live in a battlefield of good versus evil. We hear voices coming in from all sorts of directions: the TV, our neighbor, our boss, our mom, our children, the Bible, the in-laws, etc. There is an onslaught of voices in our days. We process. Then we choose. This is our daily mental battleground of activity. I call it "the voices and the choices," or "the battle of the WILLS." These four wills are:

1. **The will of God the Father**. God designed each of us ON purpose, WITH purpose, and FOR a purpose. He is the Creator, the Knitter, and the Knower. We are fearfully and wonderfully made. God designed that we walk in harmony with His plan.

2. **The will of the enemy**. We have an enemy—a thief, who comes to rob, kill, and destroy us. He seeks death over life and has purposed to destroy all that is good and right. The battle is on!

3. **Our own self will**. Then we have to deal with our own self-will, our own selfish nature, and our own pride that wants our own way. Hormones in adolescence show up as a rising of this self-will. This is normal as we develop our own identity.

4. **The will of the other**. This could be parents, a teacher, boss, or pastor. There are often many voices in our lives telling us what to do. Most of these voices mean well, but they are still other voices to contend with during formative teen years.

After watching this battle in my life for over half a century, I have come to realize that I don't even want my will, my way, or the consequences that are attached. In the same spirit of Jesus, we say, "Not my will, but Thine, be done." We know that His plan is greater than what we could hope or imagine. My best choice is God's will in God's way.

The Lord wants our teens to mature into adulthood and into greater usefulness. The enemy fights to bring confusion during this transition.

Let's be aware of the battlefield and lean in to hear His voice over the voices of all others.

Ponder:

How can I become more aware of the battlefield of the voices and the choices going on in my mind each day? Ponder how to share this concept with your children. Invite them to choose His voice above all the noise.

Scripture:

Matthew 6:33

But seek first His kingdom and His righteousness, and all these things will be given to you as well.

John 10:10

The thief comes only to steal and kill and destroy; I have come that they may have life and have it to the full.

Prayer:

Lord, I want to hear Your voice above the noise of my life. I want Your will, Your way. Help me see the choices clearly and decide wisely. I will love my teens and pray that they hear the voice of the heavenly Father.

Day 3

Our Battle Position

*Y*ou do have an enemy, but it is not your child. It is not your people. In the heat of the battle, we need to understand the true battlefield and how to fight.

When our youngest teen sons both decided to mess around with illegal drugs, we became fearful, worried, and upset about their choices. It felt like we were fighting with our teens. There was deceit in our home. Our tone of voice projected disappointment and shame. There was a battle going on, and we thought it was us against them. However, there was an enemy coming to invade our home. Coming to rob, kill, and destroy our children.

We learned to stand and take authority over our household. We learned to ask God to bind the enemy and his work. We prayed in their bedrooms, over their decisions, over their cars, and for their friends. We were at war with an enemy who had penetrated our teens' lives. We knew where the battle was. We also understood that our teens did not understand. They were confused and couldn't possibly know the future implications of their poor choices. The enemy had blinded them.

During this often scary and heart-breaking time, we must know whom we are battling against. The Lord does not ever shame or condemn us, but He loves us and is faithful. James 1:5 states that He will give wisdom to all who ask. We decided it was better to spend more energy talking to God about our teens, than talking directly to them.

Each teen rebels in different ways. Some teens are quiet rebels who simply ignore our rules in quiet defiance. Some harbor secret sins. And some boldly do the exact opposite of what we ask. Rebellion has many forms, but there is one common denominator—the enemy. As parents, we must do battle on our knees. Our love must be wise and grace-filled. This difficult time can also bring real stress on our marriage.

Stay the course. These are our people and our God is a faithful God. Pray, pray again, and then pray some more. Seek wisdom. Do not let your heart be anxious. "Lean not on your own understanding, but in all things acknowledge Him and He will make the path straight" (Proverbs 3:5-6). Your strongest battle position is on your knees in prayer.

Ponder:

Consider how to understand the greater battle than the battle of the actions of your teen. What else could be going on?

Scripture:

Ephesians 6:12

For our struggle is not against flesh and blood, but against the rulers, against the authorities, against the powers of this dark world and against the spiritual forces of evil in the heavenly realms.

James 1:5

If any of you lacks wisdom, you should ask God, who gives generously to all without finding fault, and it will be given to you.

Prayer:

Lord, I need your wisdom to understand the real battle-ground and where to fight. Open my eyes for greater wisdom and understanding. I will love my teens and keep my battlefield position on my knees in prayer.

Day 4
Do Not Take It Personally!

I am ashamed to say that I was offended by my teens' rebellion. This was arrogance and immaturity on my part. I took their choices as a personal affront. As much as I hate to admit it, I was embarrassed. I felt like a total failure of a mom. I had never wanted my kids to hang around "them." You know, those kids who do those unacceptable things like illegal drugs. Now we were the "them" no one wanted to hang around. How very humbling!

I had attempted to be a wise mom who set boundaries, but to my children, I was a Pharisee with judgment toward "those sinners." This was a confusing time for all of us. The enemy stirred up a lot of strife in our home. My only solid ground was the Word of God and the hope I held in Him alone.

As parents, it is hard not to take our children's actions personally—but it only makes us look arrogant and selfish. We are not the center of the world. Our sin is no better than their sin. We must never throw stones at the sin of another sinner. The enemy wants us to be angry with our sinner children. Humility and compassion are our fiercest recourses, and it is only by God's strength and the power of the Holy Spirit that we can navigate this posture. Our teens come from parents who are sinners, and it is in their human nature to sin. This was such a growing time in my walk with the Lord. I learned that not only had I idolized my children, but I had idolized their behavior as well. If they behaved well, did it reflect better on me? What an arrogant thought. My personal reaction to their poor behavior made me consider that I had a lot of growing to do. I spent much time crying out to Him for wisdom.

First Corinthians 13 reminds us that love is not quick to point out sin, but to cover it. Love is humble, kind, and compassionate. It will take a fresh, moment-by-moment filling of the Holy Spirit to walk through these difficult years with the fruit of peace, patience, kindness, goodness, faithfulness, gentleness, and self-control. Come on, mom! You can do this.

Ponder:

How am I taking the behaviors of my children in a personal way? Consider how to objectively remove yourself for greater wisdom and insight.

Scripture:

Matthew 7:1-2

"Do not judge, or you too will be judged. For in the same way you judge others, you will be judged, and with the measure you use, it will be measured to you."

1 Peter 4:8

Above all, love each other deeply, because love covers over a multitude of sins.

Prayer:

Lord, I need Your help to remove my personal opinion of my child's behavior so that I can love from a greater wisdom and capacity and not from a place of personal offense. I will love my teens and pray that they hear the voice of the heavenly Father.

Day 5

Consequences Teach

*P*ain can be a great teacher ... so can consequences. Don't bail your teenagers from the natural consequences of their decisions. Let the pain reign. We often told our children, "Choices have consequences, so choose very carefully." Often it is challenging to watch our children experience the outcome of their choices. Parents often want to save their children from pain. This takes away the great lesson of "cause and effect" which runs throughout all of life. Age brings experience, and experience brings wisdom and learning. The Word of God states that trials bring about the perfecting of our character (See James 1). Well, let some of that "perfecting" begin.

Author John Maxwell writes about the importance of learning by "Failing Forward." A toddler repeatedly falls in his attempt to learn to walk; yet we would never shame him for falling. We cheer him on. As our teens fall in their attempt to grow up, we must speak life-giving truths into their hearts. Our teens need to know that we love and believe in them no matter how hard they fall. We don't love the sin, but we do love and believe in them. God shows us unconditional love. We can be a reflection of that love to our teens. This takes a lot of patience, wisdom, and maybe even some boundaries.

Our teens suffered many natural outside consequences. Some hit their pocket as we refused to pay fines or penalties that resulted from their behaviors. Jail time was a consequence. So was community service imposed by the courts.

In addition, we prayed over the consequences and boundaries that we needed to enforce as a result of their choices. The book of Proverbs is filled with wisdom about the behavior differences between the wise and the foolish. One consequence for our teens, that we chose, was to mandate a study of the book of Proverbs. We loved them and wanted them to consider the consequences of foolish living versus wise living.

In the end, our entire family was affected by our teens' choices. These were long days that we navigated "one day at a time." However, since love was at the core of all we did, this difficult chapter ultimately brought our family closer than I could have imagined. The consequences were real, but so was the love wrapped around them.

Living with the consequences of our choices teaches us to think and choose more carefully. Let the learning begin!

Ponder:

Consider the best way to allow the pain of consequences to teach your teen. What are some consequences, as a parent, that would add value to the soul of your child?

Scripture:

Galatians 6:7

Do not be deceived: God cannot be mocked. A man reaps what he sows.

James 1:2-4

Consider it pure joy, my brothers and sisters, when you face trials of many kinds, because you know that the testing of your faith produces perseverance. Let perseverance finish its work, so that you may be mature and complete, not lacking anything.

Prayer:

Lord, we know that trials can bring about the perfecting of our character. Teach me how to instruct our teens through the wisdom of appropriate consequences. I will love my teens and allow natural consequences to teach them some valuable lessons.

Day 6
Man to Man

*T*he hormones in a teen boy cause them to want to rise up and have dominion over all of THEIR earth. This is not a bad thing. It prepares them to someday lead their own family. When my boys became teenagers, they began to push me away. At first, I was deeply offended. My husband relayed something he had been reading in John Eldredge's book *Wild at Heart*. Close to the time a boy turns thirteen, moms need to step AWAY and dads need to step IN.

Most young boys want to grow up to be just like their dad ... or their image of whatever a strong adult man looks like. The hormonal boost might make them want to go out and "chop down a tree" and show off their muscles. After hormones surge in their body, they often push mom away in an effort to embrace manhood. Sometimes this is a subtle thing. Sometimes it is really obvious. And their interest in girls piques, since girls somehow no longer have cooties. This is a critical time where dads need to step in more and moms need to be aware and maybe step back. It was extremely difficult for me, but I knew they would not speak to their father as they had been speaking to me. Man code wouldn't allow such disrespect. My sons would more likely listen to him.

It is not the school's or government's responsibility to train our children. It is our responsibility. It is our duty to teach them diligently. This includes both mom and dad. The scriptures are clear that dads must pray for and engage their children in the kind of deep, heart-to-heart conversations that impart more than facts, but teach wisdom. My husband started having the difficult teen discussions. He very intentionally carved out new time to hang out and have fun with them, whether they wanted to or not. We grounded them from their compromising friends, so they had little else to do in their free time. As my husband fostered a deeper relationship WITH them, they became more secure in his LOVE for them.

Ponder:

Consider ways to get your teen sons around the influence of their father or another influential man to help guide them growing into young male adulthood. Make time and prioritize this relationship.

Scripture:

Proverbs 22:6a (NASB)

Train up a child in the way he should go...

Deuteronomy 6:6-7

These commandments that I give you today are to be on your hearts. Impress them on your children. Talk about them when you sit at home and when you walk along the road, when you lie down and when you get up.

Prayer:

Lord, I need Your help understanding testosterone. Teach me the wisdom to know the importance of the father-son relationship during my son's developmental years. I will love my teens and pray that they hear the voice of the heavenly Father.

Day 7

Outside Influences

*S*ometimes there is power in the voice of another! There was a period of time when it seemed that our rebellious teens could not (or would not) listen to us. In that season, they essentially couldn't even stand to be in the same room with us, breathing the same oxygen. This time was certainly dumbfounding. Even though we radically loved them, I will have to admit that there were certainly times that we didn't like them at all ... so to speak. We somehow weren't communicating or connecting with them on their level. Our voices were like Lucy's from the Peanuts cartoon. "Wa, wa, wa, wa, wa ..."—in one ear, out the other, no true communication.

I began to pray that God would bring other people to speak truth into their lives. Remember the "voices and choices" from Day Two of this devo series? Our teens were listening to their own voice, the enemy's voice, and their misguided friends' voices. We needed them to hear God's voice. We prayed for wisdom and for other godly adults to walk this path with them. We sought out mission trip opportunities. We sought out youth pastors. We sought out other like-hearted dads who were close to them ... Maybe an uncle ... Maybe an admired businessman or neighbor. We surrounded them with any voice of truth we could find.

The body of Christ is so important during difficult teenage years. We were grateful to be plugged into a church and life group where we could seek help. We asked others to meet with our teens and to speak truth into them—others whom they actually liked. We stayed on our knees. We remained involved in their lives. We continued to love them in ways they could understand and receive. Warm chocolate chip cookies and spaghetti were the only ministry language that they actually could hear. We fed their stomach in a search to show a love that could touch their hearts with the truth. Food became a frequent ministry item in our home. But in the end, we simply had to rest and trust for God to do His work in their lives.

Ponder:

How can you add outside positive godly influences into the lives of your teens? Encourage like-minded voices of close family friends or associates.

Scripture:

Colossians 1:9

For this reason, since the day we heard about you, we have not stopped praying for you. We continually ask God to fill you with the knowledge of His will through all the wisdom and understanding that the Spirit gives...

1 Corinthians 12:12

Just as a body, though one, has many parts, but all its many parts form one body, so it is with Christ.

Prayer:

Lord, lead us to some outside relationships that would boldly speak a common voice to build and influence our teens to live for You. I will love my teens and pray for outside influences that can speak life, truth and reason into their soul.

Day 8

Grace Upon Grace

*T*he humbling part of parenting a rebellious teen is that we begin to question ourselves. Did we teach them the truth correctly? Were we terrible parents? Did we cause their rebellious choices? Were we too hard on them? Too easy on them? Too many boundaries? Not enough boundaries? In trying to find a reason for their behavior—something we could point to in blame—the enemy comes to rob, kill, and destroy our joy.

The very best thing about coming "to the end of our rope" is that we found ourselves on our knees crying out to God. Matthew 11:28-30 became my theme. *"Come to me, all you who are weary and burdened, and I will give you rest. Take my yoke upon you and learn from me, for I am gentle and humble in heart, and you will find rest for your souls. For my yoke is easy and my burden is light."* I needed rest for my weary, confused soul. I needed grace for my children and grace for myself. I clung to the verse, *"My grace is sufficient for you, for my power is made perfect in weakness"* (2 Corinthians 12:9).

I loved these teens that I wanted to strangle. I felt so inept in knowing what to do. It was a bit like walking through a dark forest with just a flashlight in our hands. I needed grace to breathe and I needed to extend grace to immature inexperienced kids trying to navigate a critical time of life. I claimed the truth of John 15:5, *"I am the vine; you are the branches. If you remain in me and I in you, you will bear much fruit; apart from me you can do nothing."* I knew that God loved our teens more than we did. He is a trustworthy God. I was weak and needed His strength.

In the end, we learned to extend grace. We could not cast a stone. I fell more in love with our struggling sinners, even as I was still angry about the sin. I learned grace and compassion as I watched them struggle with their sin and their lack of understanding. I don't really believe that any of us try to get it wrong and totally mess up our lives. We are just blinded. We need wisdom, vision, and redemption accompanied by grace and love.

Ponder:

No one is trying to get it wrong. Consider ways that you can give yourself some extra grace to learn and then consider ways to extend some compassion and grace to your teens.

Scripture:

1 Peter 5:7

Cast all your anxiety on Him, because He cares for you.

Isaiah 40:31

But those who hope in the Lord will renew their strength. They will soar on wings like eagles; they will run and not grow weary; they will walk and not be faint.

Prayer:

Lord, You extended grace to me even while I was yet a sinner. Teach me the art of receiving Your grace and extending Your grace to myself and others. I will love my teens and extend grace in wisdom.

Day 9

Choose to Love

*T*here is never a wrong time to extend love. Our teens often felt we were judgmental, pharisaical, and narrow-minded. I didn't feel that way, but realized the enemy does whatever he can to hinder and confuse relationships. I thought we were loving and guiding. Instead of reacting to my teens' comments, I asked the Lord for the ability to slow down to really listen and love. There were times that I needed to bite my tongue and graciously walk away so that I didn't behave like a third grader in a battle I could not win. I realized the battle was not personal even when it often felt that way. The Holy Spirit opened my eyes to see past my own reactive selfishness and be able to reach out to our hurting and confused teens. In the middle of difficult conversations, I found myself saying, "Son, do you know that I love you? Do you know that you have an enemy who is trying to keep you from God's best for your life?" Then I would walk away. I knew the fight was not mine.

We intentionally worked to build and restore our relationship with our teens. Even when we didn't like them, we absolutely knew that we loved them. We sought wisdom for ways to better understand them. We found ways to laugh together. This laughter was medicine for our souls. During this crazy, confusing time, the Lord changed our relationships and did a great work in all of us. One day at a time, I learned to focus on my love of the sinner—NOT the sin. These were our children! Love won. My mother bear heart broke, but my intimacy with and trust in the Lord grew. This made me a better mother.

I began to see that they didn't understand—actually, neither did I. However, we were family, assigned by God. By God's power, I learned to love the sinners as Christ loved me. As I yielded to the work of the Holy Spirit, I learned to cover their sin with His love. This in no way altered the consequences, but I was able to see them in a clearer light—the light of the Gospel. While we were yet sinners, Christ loved us and gave Himself to die for us (See Romans 5:8).

Ponder:

Consider additional ways that you can love someone that you may not temporarily even like. Love is a choice and not a feeling. Choose love.

Scripture:

Romans 5:8

But God demonstrates His own love for us in this: While we were still sinners, Christ died for us.

Proverbs 17:22

A cheerful heart is good medicine, but a crushed spirit dries up the bones.

Prayer:

Lord, You choose to love me even while I was yet a sinner. Teach me Your ways and strengthen me with Your Spirit to do so. Help me choose love versus disappointment or anger. I will love my teens and pray that they hear the voice of the heavenly Father.

Day 10

The Death of the Vision

*T*here are blessings on the other side of brokenness. My journey through the many years of teenage rebellion changed our family in such beautiful and profound ways, I would never want to go back to the woman I was before. When you allow the Holy Spirit to navigate your days, there is a significant maturing, sanctifying process that can be had during trials and tribulations. If the trial is coming anyway, then I, absolutely, want to grow and mature as a result of it. That season of trials brought about the "perfecting of our character" as we yielded to God's work in us during the hardship. He walks with us through even our darkest days. We don't sign up for hardship but we certainly can be beautifully refined and transformed by it.

In Genesis, chapters 37-50, the Bible tells of the many "deaths of vision" Joseph walked through. God had a great plan for Joseph's life but that didn't exclude pain or suffering through loss. After Joseph's early dream/vision of his brothers bowing down, he found himself in a pit (death #1), then sold as a slave (death #2), then falsely accused (death #3), then jailed (death #4), then his clothes were ripped off (death #5), etc. But the Word makes it clear that "God was WITH Joseph." And He was orchestrating a much bigger story than Joseph could hope or imagine or understand. The journey of Joseph's story held similar truths that I clung to as I walked through my own multiple deaths of vision. My teens were not supposed to rebel. I was not supposed to be in "this pit." I thought that I had homeschooled the sin right out of them.

During this challenging time, God peeled away my grip of control over our children. I unquestionably realized that I was not in charge. My mind wrestled with this letting go. I was constantly dancing with fear and an anxious heart. Was I losing my mind? What in the heck was going on and how did we get here? Bill Johnson states, "In order to have a peace that surpasses all understanding, you have to give up your right to understand." I didn't understand. With each death of my vision, I came to rest in the knowledge that God was with me and that He was bigger than the circumstances we were going through. I was living in my own Joseph story. I was drawn into a deeper knowledge of the sovereignty of my good, good Father. I wanted His will, His way, more than ever. I did not need to understand but I did need to trust. I needed some soul rest in the hands of a trustworthy loving Father. The death of our vision is a gift if we choose to walk through it in surrender to God's greater will and purpose. Choose to trust in His greater plan and vision especially when you don't understand. This is where your hope lies.

Ponder:

Consider any "death of a vision" as an opportunity to lay down your will, your way. How could you trust God with your days and your teens as you navigate difficult times?

Scripture:

Psalm 34:18

The Lord is close to the brokenhearted and saves those who are crushed in spirit.

Deuteronomy 31:8

The Lord Himself goes before you and will be with you; He will never leave you nor forsake you. Do not be afraid; do not be discouraged.

Prayer:

Lord, I believe. Help my unbelief when I am living amidst the death of a vision that I have long gripped on to. I need to trust You are orchestrating a greater plan than just whatever I see in front of me. Teach me greater trust. I will love my teens and pray that they hear the voice of the heavenly Father.

*Y*ou will find whatever you are looking for! In 2013, I published a book titled *Are You Enough?* It includes the account of our family's journey navigating teen rebellion. We had been homeschooling our children for years. I wrote this book to encourage the heart of those that were overwhelmed and exhausted. Teenage rebellion was just one of the things one my plate. I was juggling so much for a six-year season. I found myself deeply discouraged. Rock bottom was my new normal. Where oh where was the abundant life I had dreamed of? Ann Voskamp's book, *One Thousand Gifts: A Dare to Live Fully Right Where You Are,* challenged me to begin searching for and writing down "the praiseworthy" in my life. This gratitude journal launched me on a transformative journey that has proved to be a life-giving antidepressant for my life.

As the story goes, the vulture looks for death and decay and the hummingbird looks for life and nectar. They both find what they seek. We find what we are looking for as well. The enemy of darkness wants us to focus on the negative; our have-nots. But God's Word tells us to be grateful and focus on "that which is praiseworthy"—on our blessings and gifts.

It makes me really mad that our enemy comes to "rob, kill, and destroy" my joy. But what makes me even madder is that I participate and willingly give it up. Satan is subtle, cunning, and sneaky. If he can get us to whine and complain about our circumstances, then he has taken our joy. Or rather—we have given it to him. How we respond and where we choose to focus is our choice.

As I yielded my tough circumstances to God, He helped me learn to "give thanks in all things." He opened my eyes to see the good around me. This was the oxygen that I needed for my weary soul. The practice of gratitude is a life-giving habit that now helps me better navigate trials. We must simply choose to reframe our circumstances to find the good.

Even in the midst of the rebellion around me, I asked God to open my eyes and show me His gifts. It was a daily treasure hunt. This habit has become a true game-changer in my life. Whenever depression or doubt rear their ugly heads, I grab my gratitude journal, open my heart and eyes, and record His abundant gifts to me. May gratitude change your heart and your thinking. For me, seeking all that is praiseworthy was critical for a life of JOY.

Ponder:

Consider a treasure hunt for all the blessings amidst your days. You can look for the silver-lining even if your life feels burdened and heavy. Blessings are everywhere for the eyes that can see them.

Scripture:

Philippians 4:8

Finally, brothers and sisters, whatever is true, whatever is noble, whatever is right, whatever is pure, whatever is lovely, whatever is admirable—if anything is excellent or praiseworthy—think about such things.

Psalm 100:4

Enter His gates with thanksgiving and His courts with praise. Give thanks to Him, bless His name.

Prayer:

Lord, I ask Your Holy Spirit to help open my eyes to see the blessings around me. I want to obey Your word to focus on and seek all that is praiseworthy. I need You Lord! I will love my teens and pray that they hear Your voice.

*D*uring the difficult teenage chapter of my life there was an on-slaught of other things simultaneously happening. While my teens were lying, my parents were dying. We were in a deep financial valley and I was very menopausal just to name a few. I was so over-whelmed. I was definitely at the proverbial "end of my rope." It was a difficult, beautiful, stripping, exhausting time.

In my attempts to have a grateful heart, I wrote: "Thank you Lord for wanting my whole heart, my whole mind and my whole soul … so much … that you would strip everything away and leave me with a sweet emptiness that demands that I lay at rest in Your arms." This new perspective of His total Holy pursuit of me brought a deep rest and peace. It quieted my spirit with a new point of view. I decided to choose to "lay at rest in His arms." I was personally exhausted. I gave up the battle. I surrendered to "Not mine, but Thine" once again. I decided to rest and trust.

By nature, I am a verbal processor. However, in my rest, I stopped talking as much and started praying more. I became tired of words and just wanted to be held by a good, good God who was revealing Himself to me as a good, good Father. I was able to respond to the heartache—within and without—with a deep rest in my soul.

This started a beautiful season of prayer, trust, and intimacy. I prayed about everything and trusted God to hear. I refused to enter a battle that I could not win. I trusted His timing. Wisdom taught me to qui-etly accept this deep rest. The battle was too draining.

Do you find yourself at the "end of the rope"? This is a good place to be if it leads your control-freak nature to a beautiful surrender in the Lord. This can be a transforming place where humility and weakness reveal His true strength and purposes for your life. It is a place of real freedom.

Ponder:

How can you develop a habit of talking to God more and to your people less? Consider His pursuit to bring you to a place of rest and trust. Let go and let God.

Scripture:

Philippians 4:6-7

Do not be anxious about anything, but in every situation, by prayer and petition, with thanksgiving, present your requests to God. And the peace of God, which transcends all understanding, will guard your hearts and your minds in Christ Jesus.

Matthew 18:19-20

"Again, truly I tell you that if two of you on earth agree about anything they ask for, it will be done for them by My Father in heaven. For where two or three gathers in my name, there am I with them."

Prayer:

Lord, I want less talking and more praying. I need to talk to You and remind myself that You are trustworthy. I need rest. Help me trust You at new levels. I will love my teens and pray that they hear Your voice.

Day 13

My Solid Ground

*I*s there such a thing as solid ground in a shaky world? I need some of that! During the confusing days of teenage rebellion, I was scrambling for some solid ground of assurance. I felt like such a failure of a mom. How was this story going to end? When does the craziness stop? What could I count on? Only God's word is trustworthy. My only solid ground was to count on His promises to be true. What God says He will do, He will do. I hung on to His promises. I hung on for dear life.

However, there were times when it felt as if God had failed us. Did He really know what was going on in our household? How long was long enough to wait on an answer to prayer? Very often in the midst of our grief and brokenness, we do not see the bigger picture. We cannot know what God is doing. We are restlessly impatient.

Scripture affirms that God never fails. His Word is the same yesterday, today, and forever. In times of desperation and grief, we must remember that we may not be seeing God's good and gracious purpose from our current vantage point. This is when we have to trust in His promises. He knows what is going on from all angles. We do not have the mind of God or His eternal perspective. That is where I rested.

When we feel faithless or hopeless and when we believe that God has left us, we must take refuge in His Word. It has withstood the test of time. Let it be our shield. Let it be our source of protection. Ask Him to bring His Word alive in your heart. His promises can be fully trusted no matter what our circumstances may be.

I loved God and trusted Him to work "all things together for good" in our family (See Romans 8:28). I counted on Him to make "beauty from ashes" and to "restore what the locust had eaten" (See Isaiah 61:3 and Joel 2:25). I needed His "mercies to be new every morning" and

His "strength to sustain me in my weakness" (See Lamentations 3:22-23 and 2 Corinthians 12:9).

These scriptures become my lifeline of hope, rest, and peace. I couldn't trust my teens. Heck, I couldn't even trust myself. I memorized scripture. I came to a resting place where I chose a quiet resolve and a confident trust in the Trustworthy One. His Word and His promises were the solid ground in my shaky world.

Ponder:

Who are you trusting? Where is your solid ground? The Word says that He cannot fail us. Have you considered trusting a trustworthy God who loves you enough to redeem your life? Memorize His promises.

Scripture:

Romans 8:28

And we know that in all things God works for the good to those who love Him, who have been called according to *His* purpose.

2 Samuel 7:28

Sovereign Lord, You are God! Your covenant is trustworthy, and You have promised these good things to Your servant.

Prayer:

Lord, I need solid ground in my shaky world. I want to believe that Your promises are true. Help my unbelief. I need You. I will love my teens and pray that they hear Your voice and come to stand on your promises.

Day 14

This is Only a Test

*I*s this a test or an invitation? As a kid, on TV, I remember hearing the annoying "This is a test. This is only a test of the Emergency Broadcast System." I often hear a still, small voice that says something similar to me: "This is a test. This is only a test. If you can pass this test, I have greater things for you." Scripture confirms that if we will be faithful in the small things, He will trust us with greater things.

I came to realize that God was pursuing me through everything including my difficult times. He had more for me. I was living far below my Christian privilege as a believer. He used this season to draw me to Him. It was a difficult yet beautiful time of surrender. Desperation took me to surrender, but Love lifted me up and met me. I became stronger and wiser. I got better instead of bitter.

I could see that He was beckoning me to something richer and deeper than the treadmill of busyness and performance that this world offered. I was hungry for more. The intimate love relationship that He offers is like none other. When I am totally enraptured in His love, wholeness, and purposes, then my "other people" fade in the background. I find that His love spills out of my intimate relationship with Him and into the lives of those I love.

Realizing that my FIRST purpose is to know HIM and His love for me, I decided to enter into a rich slow dance with Jesus. I needed to slow down my world and enter into an unfailing deep love relationship.

In a slow dance we are close and intimate.

In a slow dance we can hear His whisper.

In a slow dance He is holding us on solid ground.

In a slow dance we are together.

In a slow dance He is carrying us with His strength.

In a slow dance His love is completely satisfying.

He in me, and I in Him. Through my trials, He invited me into an intimacy with the Knitter, the Knower, the Redeemer, the Restorer. Nothing else satisfies. All other relationships pale in comparison.

Slow down. Breathe. Enter into the tender slow dance of intimacy with Him—your holy and safe Secret Place.

Ponder:

Experiences bring wisdom and strength. How have you allowed the tests in your life to develop a greater capacity for love, strength, wisdom, and intimacy?

Scripture:

James 4:8a

Come near to God, and He will come near to you...

Jeremiah 33:3

Call to Me and I will answer you and will tell you great and unsearchable things you do not know.

Prayer:

Lord, I want to pass the test of little things to be given more and greater things. I want to grow up into Your greater purposes and plans for my life. I will love my teens and pray that they hear Your voice.

CHAPTER 15

Finding Rest for My Soul

*H*ow does rest sound? Soul rest? The kind of rest that doesn't require crash naps, screaming into pillows in your car, and binging cat videos on YouTube to escape reality? I mean, a heart of rest that prevails no matter the storms of life? We can have it—all we have to do is receive it from the One who gives it.

Even though I wrote this chapter in the utter chaos that was 2020, it felt like a not-so-distant memory of similar seasons of chaos throughout my life. During one of those seasons, I decided that "rest" was going to be the defining word of my year. I tried to turn off the calendar, the dings and the duties, to make myself sit near a window and "rest." Turns out the act of resting your body does no good if your spirit is still spinning. By God's grace, I learned for the first time what it means to experience deep and true soul rest. I want to invite you in.

Day 1

Soul Rest

*F*or those of us that operate in fifth gear, we have to work really hard at trying to rest. Are you kidding me? Even when my body is at rest my mind is usually still racing. My word for the year a few years back was the word "REST." I never worked so hard at trying to rest. It was like a comedy routine. First, rest is defined "to cease work or movement in order to relax, refresh oneself, or recover strength." A second definition is "to be placed or supported so as to stay in a specified position."

In alignment with the first definition, I started limiting my calendar commitments. In order to seek this elusive rest, I practiced sitting and staring out a window with spare time for thinking. Much to my disappointment, my racing mind would think about all the things that I was not accomplishing by sitting there. Even if I was sitting still, my mind was running at full pace ahead on the mental treadmill. Thinking that my identity was in my performance, I had historically filled my days with activity. I was doing so much "good for God" and could prove it to Him with my busy calendar. My performance mentality led to a life full of exhaustion.

So, then I moved to the second definition: "to be placed or supported so as to stay in a specified position." I definitely wanted to live from a new position, a position of DEEP rest within my soul. I wanted this "specified position!" This would require me to live from a greater level of trust in the TRUSTWORTHY One. I could not live from my performance treadmill any longer. I was too tired. I needed to live FROM God's Holy Spirit power within, rather than live FOR God from who I am and what I could do. This would be a game-changer for my days as my rest and my hope comes from Him alone. I had to learn that my sweet Lord didn't actually desire my performance but a rich relationship with me. It continues to be a great "letting go" so that I can hold on to my new soul rest and peace of mind. It reflects a great paradox of a dying to live. A place of freedom and peace … soul rest.

Ponder:

How can you identify whether you live FROM Him or FOR Him? One place is peaceful, and one place is exhausting. Ponder deep soul rest from a rich relationship of trusting the Trustworthy One.

Scriptures:

Exodus 33:14

The Lord replied, "My Presence will go with you, and I will give you rest."

Psalm 62:5

Yes, my soul, find rest in God; my hope comes from Him.

Prayer:

Oh Lord, help me find my soul rest in You alone. Help me empty myself of myself so that You can live through me instead of me living FOR You. I will tether my soul rest and my peace of mind to Your character and faithfulness.

Day 2

Choosing Trust

*D*o we really trust God to be God? Is He a good God? There is a freedom and rest on the other side of surrendering to these truths and choosing to trust them. Do we really want to carry the weight of the world upon our shoulders? Do we really think we can manage the behaviors and decisions of others? I often wrestle with the thought: Do I really want my will, my way? Or His will, His way? That seems like such an easy choice. It is almost impossible for this world to deliver you any "peace-of-mind" with all the news, the disappointments, and the brokenness. Since I believe in the "trash in, trash out mentality," it is imperative to spend my time meditating on the goodness and faithfulness of God versus all the problems in my life. I must choose my daily focus and can blame no one else for such. When our identity is anchored in who He is, we can find a stability beyond what our feelings dictate or suggest in the moment. When we keep our minds on Him and His promises, we can live from a greater trust which ushers in a greater peace and rest.

Will I trust that God is good? That He sees and knows things that I cannot know? Will I lean not on my own understanding of things? Will I trust Him when things are good and when things are hard? When people disappoint, betray, or reject me? When my heart gets broken or shattered? Will I trust Him with my loved ones and release control over other's behavior? Since God is good at being God, it all comes down to trust. If God is good and He is good to me, then it behooves me to choose a quiet resolve and confident trust even when I lack understanding. I lack understanding often. I have many questions for God when I get to heaven. I simply don't have His eternal perspective. Daily choosing this quiet resolve ushers in a rest and peace that could only come from my choice to let go and trust Him.

Living from a position of rest is an important component in your spiritual walk with the Lord as it allows our mind, body, and soul to renew. The control freak inside each of us demands a self-importance that is contrary to God's perfect will. Ultimately, this undercover yoke of self-importance will exhaust the best of us. He actually wants to carry our burdens and give us rest. It is time to raise the white flag of surrender and give Him our exhausted broken lives in exchange for a gentle, humble, and yielded heart, available to be used for His greater purposes. We live our best results when we are not living from our own strength and power simply trying harder and harder. Our trust brings freedom. Then we can live from the Holy Spirit of the Lord shining through us.

Ponder:

Does my control freak want to run my own show or am I willing to rest in living His will, His way each day? Consider this yielded position for His greater glory.

Scriptures:

Isaiah 26:3-4

You will keep in perfect peace those whose minds are steadfast, because they trust in You. Trust in the Lord forever, for the Lord, the Lord himself, is the Rock eternal.

Matt. 11:28-30

Come to Me, all you who are weary and burdened, and I will give you rest. Take My yoke upon you and learn from Me, for I am gentle and humble in heart, and you will find rest for your souls. For My yoke is easy and My burden is light.

Prayer:

O Lord, thank You for being willing to carry my burdens and relieve my exhausting yoke of control. Help me to choose trusting You every day … one day at a time. I will tether my soul rest and peace of mind to Your character and faithfulness.

Day 3

Sabbath Rest

*R*est is a necessity. It is a biblical principle that all creatures must rest. Without proper rest, the human body will break down. Most Christians today don't appreciate or understand the value of Sabbath rest or keeping the Sabbath day holy. Like me, most Christians live on the exhausting performance treadmill. Rest allows our mind, body, and soul to renew and restart with even more strength and focus. It is a prescription for future usefulness. Without taking time to rest, we relegate ourselves to actually being less effective in our endeavors.

The Bible makes it very clear that we are to have a Sabbath rest. There is no question about it. Wow. It is one of the Ten Commandments. We are to honor the Sabbath and pursue rest. In obedience, we simply must choose to hit the pause button, and rest. The Lord knew about our need to physically rest but also to rest in Him spiritually. We must be very intentional to guard this time! Our obedience to this command will be rewarded. Most of us do not recognize, or we underestimate, the powerful impact of Sabbath rest.

I love Lysa Terkeurst's Sabbath consideration: "It's not just a day for me to give to God. It is a day God established for me. He wants to give me something, if only I'll slow down enough to receive it." She reminds us that the Sabbath isn't a day to merely be *observed* but to be *preserved*. When we slow down and seek the Lord's rest, we can breathe and remember that it's all about God and not our own agendas. We can reflect and therefore live in His bigger story instead of living so self-centered in our own little stories.

The enemy of our souls wants us to live with an anxious unproductive heart. This will indeed limit our ministry, health, and well-being. He targets our minds. He lies to us. He does not want us to have an intentional Sabbath REST with the Lord. He wants to keep us running and exhausted. Our *busyness* is one of his greatest tools. It is the enemy's sneaky way to get us off-track and away from rest and peace, leaving us vulnerable.

God assigned our days to include Sabbath rest. He commanded such for our benefit. We need to enjoy Sabbath REST and take time to remember and refocus.

Ponder:

Ponder your obedience when it comes to the commandment to take a "Sabbath rest" even if it is not exactly on Sunday. Remember that obedience blesses us!

Scriptures:

Exodus 20:8-10

Remember the Sabbath day by keeping it holy. Six days you shall labor and do all your work, but the seventh day is a sabbath to the LORD your God. On it you shall not do any work, neither you, nor your son or daughter, nor your male or female servant, nor your animals, nor any foreigner residing in your towns.

Hebrews 4:9-10

There remains, then, a Sabbath-rest for the people of God; for anyone who enters God's rest also rests from their works, just as God did from His.

Prayer:

Lord, I need You to help me shut down the performance treadmill and embrace Your precious gift of "Sabbath rest." I want to slow down and experience Your rich Sabbath Rest. I will tether my soul rest and peace of mind to Your character and faithfulness.

Day 4

Renewing Our Mind

*D*o we have any say so in the renewing and refreshing of our minds? Certainly, we do! Figuratively speaking, the Lord wants us to walk beside quiet, life-giving waters to restore our souls. He wants to refresh our weary hearts. The Holy Spirit can do great healing work in our minds, but we must seek and invite this work. It is 100 percent a work of the Holy Spirit to bring transformative renewal, but it is 100 percent me to yield to and invite this greater work. Sadly, sometimes I think that the Lord has to "make me lie down" so that He can lead me beside the still waters that *restoreth* my soul. I rarely grab this concept on my own. Usually it happens after I have hit some sort of brick wall that stops me in my tracks. I am learning to re-frame times where I am forced to stop my plans. I now consider His greater work. I daily choose to yield my schedule to His "divine interruptions" as a way to live surrendered. This yielding is a constant reminder to let Him renew my mind toward His eternal purposes versus to my temporal daily calendar plans. Daily choose to be still and invite Him to renew your mind.

Renewing our minds is the gateway to renewing our peace of mind. Lasting peace can only come from being tethered to WHO God is and not to other people or circumstances. My peace lies in Him and not in things of this world. So, once again, I need to consider the "trash in / trash out" choices that I make each day. Do I listen to too much negativity on the news or from my "Negative Nellie" friend? Do I watch life-giving shows or trashy shows? Do I listen to the lies of the enemy or meditate on the Voice of my true identity? I am who God says I am! Who am I going to believe?

We will renew our minds from life-giving truth. I want to live in every truth of Christian promise or privilege that is afforded to me. I want to live from the mind of Christ within. I want to live in His good, pleasing, and perfect will with a mind resting in the peace of His purposes and His greater plans for my life. How about you?

Ponder:

How often do you intentionally rest for the restoration of your soul and your vision to live in a story that is greater than your own?

Scriptures:

Romans 12:2

Do not conform to the pattern of this world but be transformed by the renewing of your mind. Then you will be able to test and approve what God's will is—His good, pleasing and perfect will.

Psalm 23:1-3

The LORD is my shepherd, I lack nothing. He makes me lie down in green pastures, He leads me beside quiet waters, He refreshes my soul. He guides me along the right paths for His name's sake.

Prayer:

Lord, I need a renewed mind set on eternal truths and Your eternal purposes in each day I live. Help me not be so ME centered but live in the identity and purpose for which You have called me. I will tether my soul rest and peace of mind to Your character and faithfulness.

Day 5

Entering His Rest

*H*ow smart do we have to be to want to live from a peaceful, restful soul? The Bible says that age brings wisdom. Actually, age brings experiences and experiences bring wisdom. This includes both good and bad experiences. As long as we humble ourselves and choose to be life-long learners, wisdom can emerge like the 20/20 vision that comes from hindsight. Hindsight, as well as exhaustion, can teach us a lot if we are willing to learn. But also, we can learn from those who have gone before us and save ourselves a lot of wasted energy.

The belief that scripture is true yesterday, today, and tomorrow gives me a solid foundation upon which to stand. The Bible is His love letter TO us as well as His "owner's manual" FOR us. We are invited to an intimate relationship with our Creator, Redeemer, and Restorer, who makes all things new and offers us a peace beyond all of our own understanding, the greatest invitation for our BEST YES!

Life is filled with endless questions and uncertainty. Where is my solid ground in this shaky world? Who can I count on that does NOT disappoint, fail, or forsake me? What about these feelings that I contend with on a daily basis? Who is always with me and for me? Who can redeem and restore my messes? Where is my hope for the future? Who will love me unconditionally, no matter what? The answer is Jesus. He invites us into an intimacy that exceeds all love affairs of this world. It is the SECRET PLACE of the Most High.

This is our safe place to bow down and yield ourselves to "not mine, but Thine!" Safe in His arms, I can cast my burden upon the Lord to carry my heavy yoke. When I am at the very end of my rope, it is the best place to be if it leads me into the restful arms of my Father God. Intimacy with my Savior is like a sweet slow dance of soul rest. It is where I can find peace and safely surrender my control freak. In this secret place, I choose my quiet resolve and confident trust in the

Trustworthy ONE. No more fighting. No more carrying the weight or the burden of the load. Here I can yield to living in His bigger story and not to be wearied by my small thinking and my small living in my self-centered story. The secret place of intimacy, resting in His arms, is a place of freedom. It is free. He never fails or disappoints. This is a place where I can die to myself and yet, truly and finally live free.

You can find Him in His Word, in nature, through others, through prayer. "Seek and you shall find Him if you seek Him with all your heart" (Jeremiah 29:13). Surrender to this intimate safe place and enter a deep rest for your soul.

Ponder:

Ponder if you might be missing the sweetest relationship of your lifetime by not entering the depths of the secret place of intimacy and trust with the most high God ... a place of soul rest.

Scriptures:

Psalm 91:1

Whoever dwells in the shelter of the Most High will rest in the shadow of the Almighty.

Psalm 62:5

Yes, my soul, find rest in God; my hope comes from Him.

Prayer:

Lord, I want to have our relationship be the fuel for the rest of my days. Help me enter into all that You have for me through loving intimacy and soul rest with You. I will tether my soul rest and peace of mind to Your character and faithfulness.

CONCLUDING WORDS

*D*o you want to breathe deeply, freely, and full of joy? You cannot after achieving success with work, your kids, or your circumstances, but right now—by surrendering to the Lord and resting in him.

I lead four-day DEEPER INTENSIVE getaways for women needing to take a deep breath and get a drink of Living Water. This is a time to unplug from all the voices and noises of our world and to lean into the Voice of the One that created us, gifted us, assigned us, and numbered our days for such a time as this. One of my favorite things to watch at these intimate events is when we make personal choices to let go of things that have weighed down our lives too long and we are no longer willing to carry them into our future. We throw these things "in the fire" so to speak as we really do write them down, testify of their fleeting place, and throw them into the fire to burn forever. There are many great testimonies of freedom from past bondage that I would like to share but one in particular as we close this devotional book.

I bear witness to all the ladies who are sick and tired of "trying harder and harder." These ladies are done with carrying the "yoke of heaviness" when they are reminded that His yoke is easy, and His burden is light. They are tired of spinning plates only to have so many just fall to the ground. They are ready to finally find true rest for their souls.

> Matthew 11:29—Take My yoke on you and learn of Me; for I am meek and lowly in heart: and You shall find rest to your souls.

This soul rest does not come from a place of wrestling but from a place of resting. It comes from the impenetrable and incomprehensible mystery of "Christ in me, the hope of glory." It is time to breathe in this truth. When we grasp the truth of "exchanging our yoke" we find that our striving and trying harder ceases and our intimacy with God grows tremendously.

Life is more soul-satisfying when we are living FROM His indwelling Holy Spirit and the power given within, than it is living FOR Him in our crazy performance comparison mentality that is exhausting and totally unsustainable. Something is out of kilter if we are not living happy on our way to heaven. Are you living far below your Christian privilege?

> Colossians 1:27—To them God has chosen to make known among the Gentiles the glorious riches of this mystery, which is Christ in you, the hope of glory.

Come on, friend. Let go of your pride and control freak, and breathe from His indwelling Spirit. Live FROM Him. Let His rich Holy Spirit indwell you to an overflowing place filled with purpose. Leave the exhausting life of trying harder and harder. Leave that performance treadmill and live from a place of peace.

What does it mean to breathe and live FROM the power of God?

Living FROM Him instead of FOR Him by truly breathing fully and deeply is not about getting to a point of happiness or success where you can finally gasp for air. No. To truly breathe is to live from God's indwelling Holy Spirit breath in your heart every second of every day, no matter how suffocating circumstances may be around you. This moment by moment breathing of His indwelling Spirit is what will set you free to live from a place of rest and peace. His power is present and available at this very moment to all who believe. Your intimacy with Him will lead you to choose a life filled with the freedom of living FROM His Spirit. Let Him carry the load. Abide in him, and *breathe*!

Made in the USA
Columbia, SC
18 April 2021